t3

To John
Christp

From
Charles.

GW00648618

GREAT RACING
DISASTERS

GREAT RACING DISASTERS

John Welcome

Illustrations by Larry

Arthur Barker Limited   London

A subsidiary of Weidenfeld (Publishers) Limited

Published in Great Britain by
Arthur Barker Limited
91 Clapham High Street
London SW4 7TA

ISBN 0 213 16926 6

Photoset and printed in Great Britain by
Redwood Burn Limited
Trowbridge, Wiltshire

Contents

Preface

As anyone even remotely connected with racing knows, in this sport triumph and disaster are the closest of bedfellows. This little book deals with disasters not triumphs, but care, we are told, sits behind the horseman and disaster of one sort or another is never far away from even the most triumphant of stables and most successful of owners. When disaster strikes it does so ruthlessly without regard to person or prestige and all the sufferer can do is to repeat the classic words 'that's racing' and reflect that horses were born to make fools of men.

These disasters, on and off the racecourse, come in many guises and I have tried to show that they are not unique to the present day by going back into history. Some arise from human folly – never more evident perhaps than on the racecourse; some from the idiosyncrasies of that noble animal around which the whole sport revolves; some from envy, greed and all uncharitableness typified by the trials and tribulations to which the then Prince of Wales, afterwards Prince Regent, and Bob Sievier were subjected by their peers.

I have tried to mingle the serious with the light-hearted – with the latter, I hope, predominating, for it is a light heart, or at least the ability to take hard knocks with a light heart, which is a prerequisite without which no one in racing, be he punter, owner, trainer, rider or, indeed, steward, can expect to survive.

It is this ability either successfully to endure or to laugh at disaster which I hope runs through this book. Such sang-froid is especially associated with the amateur tradition. Roddy Owen and the brothers Brown had it in abundance, as had

Quinny Gilbey and that greatest of modern Corinthians, Lord Mildmay. The Marquis of Hastings, 'Mad Harry' alas, did not, and perished through its lack.

Many of their stories are described in this book along with betting coups which have gone astray, races lost that might have been won, plots failed and stratagems aborted. I trust they may serve to pass an idle hour between studies of form, or lighten a despondent report from trainer or jockey as to a horse's progress or lack of it; even, perhaps, to help brighten the grisly moments of settling day.

JOHN WELCOME
April 1985

1 Royalty, Reformers and Rakes

'If Chifney continues to ride your Royal Highness's horses no gentleman will start against them.' Such was the extraordinary injunction sent by Sir Charles Bunbury, then senior steward of the Jockey Club and one of his future subjects, to the heir to the throne in the year 1791.

It all arose out of the running of the Prince's horse, Escape, at the Newmarket October Meeting of that year, and it precipitated consequences which Sir Charles can scarcely have anticipated when he penned that ill-judged and insolent missive.

Bunbury was a hasty, opinionated and domineering man. His wife, who ran away from him after five years of marriage and whom he subsequently divorced, obtaining an Act of Parliament to do so, castigated him as dull, sententious and a bore. There is no doubt, however, that the conduct of the Prince and his jockey, Chifney, during their careers on the Turf had gone a long way towards alienating those anxious to preserve the proprieties and uphold moral standards amongst whom Sir Charles, possibly because of his own broken marriage, was one of the principals.

The Prince then, as always, liked the louche and picked his favourites from the fast set. His principal crony at that time was Sir John Lade. A nephew of Dr Johnson's friend, Henry Thrale, Lade had been instrumental in introducing the learned Doctor to the Turf and fostering in him a lifelong fascination with it though also, perhaps because of Lade, he perceived its blemishes and went so far in his dictionary as to define a jockey as 'a cheat, a trickish fellow'. In any event, Lade's intellectual pretensions went no further than his acquaintanceship with the Doctor for horses and gambling took up his whole life. A superb whip, he could handle anything 'from a four-in-hand to a mule cart' and once won a bet that he could drive both off wheels of his coach over a sixpenny bit. He would, in fact, bet on anything and the more extravagant and outrageous the bet the better he liked it, as when he took on the Duke of Queensberry, 'Old Q', of whom we shall hear again, that his champion would eat more in a given time than the Duke's contender. He lost this bet by 'a pig and an apple pie' and the contest once more had outraged the proprieties.

The final flaunting of the social order and niceties by Lade came with his marriage to Letitia Darley, the widow of Sixteen String Jack, a highwayman who had been hanged at Tyburn. Letty Lade could handle 'the ribbons' as well if not better than any of the famous whips of the day including her husband and hold her own with them too, in her command of foul language acquired from her highwayman consort. When, soon after the marriage, the Prince danced with her at an Assembly at Brighton the leading ladies of the gathering left the room. Those few of the great ladies of the day who went racing shunned her or, to use her own words, 'made vulgar mouths' at her on the racecourse.

None of these things deterred the Prince. The trio were everywhere together, the fair Letty with a feather in her hat, the Prince and Lade decked out in the full fig of early Georgian male splendour. They enjoyed themselves hugely and scandalised the staid. Altogether it is not surprising that when the whole entourage, including sundry hangers-on, appeared at Newmarket that October, censorious and disdainful looks were directed at them and that anything irregular in the running and riding of the Prince's horses was likely to be the subject of the closest scrutiny. This was all the more probable since the Prince's career on the Turf had hitherto been one of unalloyed success which had engendered both envy and jealousy in certain high quarters.

His jockey, Chifney, too, though a very great rider, had become thoroughly spoilt by royal patronage. His conceit in his own abilities knew no bounds; worse still he took no trouble to conceal it, which did not endear him to the rulers of the Turf led by Bunbury.

From the Prince's point of view matters went awry from the very start of the meeting since, although he was unaware of it, Chifney, who thought he knew everything not only about riding but also about training racehorses, was in the process of having a row with Mr Lake, the Prince's trainer.

Escape was a stayer with little turn of foot and was not an easy horse either to ride or train. He needed a lot of work and he needed a distance of ground. At a previous meeting Chifney had won on him twice over four miles; he was of the opinion that he knew more about him than Lake and was not hesitant about expressing that opinion. Further, when he saw him stripped he said that he did not look ready to run and was short of 'a sweat'. He also thought – and said – that the distance of two miles in the Sixty Guineas Stakes which he was due to run next day was too short for him. These exchanges, it need hardly be remarked, did not endear him to Lake.

From the start it fell out exactly as Chifney had foretold. Escape never got into the race at all and finished last. After he had weighed in, Chifney went to the Prince and said to him that the race would have brought Escape on, that if they ran him the following day over his true distance, four miles, he was sure to win and suggested that the Prince should back him. Once more he was proved right for win Escape did, beating in the process two horses which had finished in front of him the day before. Then the fur began to fly.

Hardly had the horses passed the post when Lake, furious with Chifney's aspersions on his training, went to the Prince and said: 'I give Your Royal Highness joy, but I am sorry the horse has won. I would sooner have given a hundred guineas and seen him beaten for it sounds very bad.'

Lake was not the only one to make such comments. Stories inspired by envy, malice and financial loss flew about Newmarket and became magnified as they went. The wildest of all, though it gained credence amongst those willing to believe any-

11

thing of the Prince and his circle, was that he himself had been seen stealing, bucket in hand, into Escape's stable an hour or so before the race to give him a copious drink of water and so stop him!

Hearing of these stories and suggestions the Prince had Chifney summoned to his presence. There he cross-examined him with severity as to the race and his riding in it, and it must be remembered that the Prince knew racing and was no mean judge of it. At the end of the cross-examination he expressed himself satisfied that no wrong had been done and that he accepted Chifney's explanation.

Bunbury, however, was far from satisfied. Having watched the race and heard the rumours he was horrified; he may well, also, have seen in all these things an opportunity of teaching the Prince and, more importantly, Chifney, a lesson. He called Chifney to explain his riding to himself and his brother stewards and, according to reports, took over the conduct of the enquiry himself, grilling Chifney for upwards of half an hour. Chifney stuck to his guns and his explanation that the first race had been all wrong for the horse and the second all right. Bunbury failed to get an agreement from his fellows to condemn him and no official reprimand was ever issued by the Jockey Club either to the Prince or Chifney. Bunbury, however, for reasons known only to himself was still not satisfied. He was still smouldering, still disbelieving and still hell-bent, apparently, on having Chifney punished and, perhaps, through him, his master. He returned home and solely on his own initiative, wrote that ill-advised letter to the Prince the consequences of which, as has been said, he could hardly have envisaged.

For disaster to all concerned struck immediately.

On receiving the letter the Prince was furious. Never before during his successful career on the Turf had the riding or running of one of his horses been questioned. The letter was an insult and he was not prepared to lie down under it. Forthwith he set about showing Bunbury what Royal disfavour could do. First he summoned Chifney to his presence and, to demonstrate his confidence in him, he let it be known that he had told

12

. . . the Prince had been seen stealing, bucket in hand, into Escape's stable an hour or so before the race . . .

him: 'You have been an honest and good servant to me, Sam Chifney, and you shall be paid two hundred guineas a year from my funds so long as I shall live.' Next he announced that because of the insult offered him he was withdrawing from the Turf, dispersing the bloodstock and, moreover, would never, either as owner or spectator, set foot in Newmarket again.

Bunbury was appalled; this was far more than he had bargained for. The withdrawal of royal patronage hit Newmarket hard. The standard of racing declined and attendances fell off. Bunbury then panicked. Unofficially, in an effort to mend the rift, he saw to it that the Prince was informed that the authorities wanted him back. It did not work. A little later Chifney met His Royal Highness on the Steyne at Brighton, and, telling him this, asked if there was any hope of his return. 'Sam Chifney,' the Prince answered. 'There has never been a proper apology made and they used you and me very ill. They are bad people. I'll not set my foot on the ground any more.'

Later, when the Prince did return to racing in a smaller way, Bunbury, now doubly regretting the results of his hasty action and the ill effects it had had on his stewardship and the sport, ate a large portion of humble pie. He led a deputation to the Prince and presented a petition couched in the most grovelling tones asking that the Escape affair might be forgotten and that Newmarket 'might again be honoured by Your Royal Highness's condescending attendance'. The Prince in his genial way agreed to consider the matter but he did not return nor did he forget. Years later when Chifney's son William asked him if he would then change his mind he received the reply: 'No, no, William, they treated your poor father and I very badly. I won't run there.' The wound went too deep.

Some few years before the Escape scandal, the Duke of Queens-

14

berry, when the Earl of March, had put himself in peril of his life over a piece of sharp practice on the racecourse.

Sir Ralph Gore, a cavalry officer stationed at the Curragh in County Kildare, had brought with him to Ireland a useful horse of which he thought a great deal called Black and All Black. Matched against a mare called Irish Lass to the great disappointment of his owner, Black and All Black was well beaten, the populace ascribing Irish Lass's comfortable victory to the fact that she wore a rosary round her neck during the race.

The Earl of March was also in Ireland at the time and he too had brought a good horse with him. This was Bajazet who had already made a name for himself in England by winning over distances from two to six miles. Now the Earl of March had him in Ireland looking for further pickings which he was never averse to accumulating where and when he could.

March, later to become notorious as 'Old Q, the Star of Piccadilly', gamester and seducer of or attempted seducer of anything in skirts that came near him, was already earning for himself the reputation of taking such precautions as were necessary either within or without the rules to see that his wagers were winning ones. Some of these were ingenious in the extreme as when he bet an opponent he could convey a letter fifty miles in an hour, a feat on the face of it impossible in those days. March placed the letter inside a cricket ball, hired a team of twenty-four skilled catchers who threw it from hand to hand over a measured distance, and easily collected his bet.

Casting about for a likely winning bet March observed the defeat of Black and All Black. He did not share the belief that this was due to heavenly intervention produced by the rosary and he proposed a match between him and Bajazet. Sir Ralph, anxious to restore the prestige of his horse, readily agreed. The terms were a prize of a thousand guineas – a sum well worth winning in those days – Black and All Black to carry 10st and Bajazet 10st 7lb. On the face of it these weights appeared to favour Black and All Black but Bajazet had carried no less than 12st when winning over six miles in England. Nevertheless it seems that March was not altogether happy about the weight

March placed the letter inside a cricket ball, hired a team of twenty-four
skilled catchers who threw it from hand to hand over a measured distance . . .

concession. He could probably have done the weight himself for he was in those early days a proficient gentleman rider but he chose to put up a professional who would have to carry lead. For this purpose he had a 'shotten belt' made with pouches in it into which the lead was placed and which was buckled round the jockey's waist when he went to scale. The construction and method of wearing this belt gave obvious opportunities of jettisoning it either before or during the race, a fact which there seems no doubt March had taken into account. In the event that is what happened, the jockey handing the belt to an accomplice on the way out and collecting it on the way in. In fact the ruse profited its progenitors not at all for despite the trickery over the weights Black and All Black won the match easily.

Sir Ralph Gore was a hot-tempered man. It was said of him once when dining at Newmarket he had thrown a waiter whom he deemed to be impertinent through the window nearest to his table. When the landlord ventured a timid protest he received the reply: 'Damn your eyes, sir, put the fellow on the bill!' He was, too, well aware of March's reputation; he had been suspicious of him from the first and had kept a close watch on his jockey. The handing out of the belt had been quickly and cleverly managed but its return was botched and Sir Ralph spotted the trickery. Immediately he had the jockey and his accomplice brought before him. Under his fierce questioning the terrified jockey pleaded that he was only obeying instructions and that the whole fraud had sprung from the fertile brain of the Earl of March. Sir Ralph lost no time in calling out the noble Earl to face him at dawn with pistols for two.

March, it is hardly necessary to say, did not care at all for this outcome. He had lost his money and now looked likely to lose his life for Sir Ralph was a crack shot. It was said of certain regiments then stationed in Ireland that the first question asked of an officer newly posted to them was, 'Does he blaze?' The reply in Sir Ralph's case would certainly have been in the affirmative for he had already 'blazed' with some success and

. . . he had a 'shotten belt' made with pouches in it into which the lead was placed and buckled round the jockey's waist . . .

was believed to have killed three of his opponents. The same could not have been said of the Earl of March who was only notable for the ingenuity of the excuses he manufactured to avoid the results of his sly stratagems. But here he was cornered for the challenge had been made in public in front of the 'stand house' at the Curragh and before most of the nobility and gentry of Ireland.

As may be imagined March spent an anxious time while the formalities were being arranged but, to the surprise of some, he did turn up at the appointed time and hour bringing with him his second and, as an added precaution, a surgeon.

In addition to his hot temper Sir Ralph was possessed of a macabre sense of humour and he was well aware of his adversary's disinclination to face powder and shot. He timed his arrival at the duelling ground to be later than that of March and when he appeared was seen to be heading a small procession. Behind him were two servants carrying a large, highly polished, black box about the length of a man. It was, in fact, a coffin.

Beckoning the servants up, Sir Ralph instructed them to place the box at March's feet. When he looked down March saw that the lid of the box was emblazoned with his coat of arms with, below it, the inscription: 'William Douglas, Earl of March, who departed this life on the 10th day of June 1757' – the very day on which the antagonists were about to face each other.

It was recorded by the observers that, on reading the inscription, March blanched and appeared to be about to faint. He did, however, summon up enough courage to enquire of Gore the meaning of the charade whereupon Sir Ralph blandly replied: 'My dear fellow, you are, of course, aware that I never miss my man, and, as I feel myself in excellent form this morning, I have not a shadow of doubt in my mind but that this oaken box will shortly be better calculated for you than your present dress.'

That finished whatever fight was left in March. He immediately confessed that he had been the author of the fraud and

'My dear fellow, you are, of course, aware that I never miss my man . . .'

made a full, ingratiating and ample apology. He left the field of
honour – disgraced.

There is a postscript to this story. Disgrace sat lightly on
March throughout his life. Although there was talk of compel-
ling him to resign from his clubs and some cut him in the street
nothing further was in fact done for he was an adept at brazen-
ing things out. Duelling was beginning to be frowned on in
England and it was widely held that the Irish regiments and
gentry had too ready a recourse to the 'saw-handles'. March
was able to capitalise on these sentiments and to claim himself a
pioneer of a more civilised method of settling disputes. It was
not long before he succeeded in having himself elected to the
Jockey Club and one of his first actions was to write a long
paper on the paramount importance of jockeys carrying the
correct weights!

Roguery and vice of all sorts raged unchecked on the Turf in
those early formative days. From the highest to the lowest no
one was exempt and, as we have seen, certain members of the
Jockey Club scarcely set a prime example. Indeed Bunbury
himself, that self-appointed pillar of virtue, was far from being
above suspicion regarding the running of certain of his horses
moving Nimrod the celebrated sporting recorder and reporter
to write of two such occasions : 'In both these cases money was
lost. The question is, who won it?'
Lord George Bentinck, who succeeded Bunbury as dictator

of the Turf, set himself out to change all this. The trouble about Lord George was that he was in character rude, arrogant and over-bearing. He fought with almost everyone with whom he came in contact and he made more enemies than most men have friends.

Although he could see the motes in others' eyes he was quite incapable of perceiving them in his own. He pursued iniquity in lesser men, yet, like Bunbury before him, he was none too scrupulous about the running of his own horses and his gambling was on a positively herculean scale. 'He counted the thousands won after a great race as a general would count his prisoners and his cannon after a great victory', one chronicler recorded but he added the telling rider: 'His tricks and stratagems he regarded as the tactics by which his success was achieved.' His cousin, George Greville, the diarist, with whom he quarrelled most bitterly, wrote of him after he had exposed one fraud: 'What a humbug it all is and if everyone knew what I knew of his tactics and artifices what a humbug he would be thought!'

He very nearly lost his life in a duel with 'Squire' Osbaldeston, one of the best pistol shots in England – he could put ten shots into the ace of spades at thirty paces – whom he had recklessly insulted over a bet and who declared to a friend on the eve of the meeting: 'I'll shoot the beggar dead tomorrow morning or rather today for it's after midnight.' In fact, Lord George's life was only saved by the intervention of that friend, George Payne, a man known and loved by all the racing world, a born diplomat and a patcher up of quarrels.

There is no denying, however, that Lord George did much to cleanse the Turf of its worst abuses and malpractices. One of the most heinous of these was the prevalence of a crude form of doping to 'nobble' or stop a horse in his race which in actuality often amounted to fatal poisoning. Indeed, shortly before Lord George came on the scene, White's betting book recorded a wager of five guineas, 'That destroying a horse by poisoning is not a capital offence by Act of Parliament.' This wager was ultimately settled by the apprehension in the act of a man called Dawson, the leader of a gang of dopers or poisoners, and his hanging by the neck until he was dead in Cambridge Castle.

Lord George's most celebrated campaign was, of course, his exposure of the Running Rein fraud when the winner of the Derby of 1844 was proved to have been a four-year-old and his pursuit and bringing to justice of the miscreants who carried it out.

This success, coupled with the persistence, acumen and attention to detail with which he carried it out, rightly earned for Lord George a unanimous vote of thanks from the Jockey Club though the judge at the subsequent trial acidly remarked: 'If gentlemen condescend to race with blackguards they must condescend to expect to be cheated.'

These remarks may well have been inspired not only by the Running Rein case but by another racing scandal which occurred a few days later and which by becoming public property had a near disastrous effect on the honour of the Turf such as it then was and which Lord George was so anxious to preserve.

Crockford, the owner of the gambling hall in St James's Street and another gambler along with confederates on a momentous scale owned Ratan, the second favourite in Running Rein's Derby. On the morning of the race Ratan received a dose which was intended either to dope or poison him but the gang got the mixture wrong and it did not take effect so, to make assurance doubly sure, they bribed his jockey to stop him which he duly did. Crockford was ill in bed at the time and when the news of all this was conveyed to him it so affected him that it brought on an attack of apoplexy from which he died two days later – on the morning of the Oaks in fact.

Crockford and his syndicate had backed the filly Princess in the Oaks to win them an immense sum of money but by the rules then pertaining death cancelled all bets. The members of the syndicate, regarding Princess as a certainty, conceived a way to avoid cancellation and to collect their winnings. One of their members was sent to Epsom with a carrier pigeon in a basket. He was instructed to answer all enquiries as to Crockford's health by saying that he was in the club, well enough but eagerly awaiting the result of the race – hence the pigeon.

Princess duly won and the pigeon was released. The gang then carried out the second part of their plan. They dressed the corpse, brought it downstairs and placed it in the bow window of Crockford's overlooking St James's Street. There it sat, a ghastly rictus of a smile on its face, surveying the scene, mute evidence of the living existence of its owner.

Many of those returning from Epsom would, as the confederates well knew, pass down St James's Street in their carriages, and were sure to glance up at the windows of Crockford's to see how the old man was faring. This was, in fact, just what happened and the general acceptance was that Crockford was, despite reports, not only still living but fit and well. One gentleman indeed reported him as being 'quite lively'! The bets were collected but the story was too good to remain untold. Someone talked; the secret was out. The honour of the Turf was once more in disastrous disrepute.

Stories such as these only served to spur Lord George on but he had his setbacks, two of which could have been disastrous, the one to his pocket the other to his prestige, although the latter did bring disaster to his adversary as well.

The arrogance with which Lord George conducted himself especially towards those whom he regarded as lesser mortals approached at times megalomania but he met his match when he tangled with a wild Irishman called Thomas Ferguson. One who knew Ferguson well has described him: 'He was affected with a violent, and at times, ungovernable temper, which could not brook opposition, much less what he considered injustice and when he met with such he would give way to paroxysms of rage unrestrained in violence. This infirmity

One gentleman indeed reported him as being 'quite lively'!

made him many enemies and brought him constantly into trouble for he cared not for class or person. In fact, the more exalted in station the man might be who provoked him, the more terrible was Tom's scathing vituperation.'

Having that character it was to be expected that when he and Lord George clashed sparks would fly, and they did.

'Choleric Tom', as he was sometimes known, had an outstanding colt called Harkaway with whom he cheated most scandalously according to the state of his pocket and his betting book. Finding that he had plundered Irish racing until it could stand no more – 'There is nothing left here to cheat', he told a friend – he brought Harkaway to England. The colt's first big win in this country was the Goodwood Cup when, giving weight all round, and far from fit, he slammed a good field. Goodwood was Lord George's favourite course. When he first entered racing he had had his horses trained there; he never missed a meeting and it was due to his efforts that it became one of the leading courses in the country. It was inevitable then that his sharp eye should fall on Harkaway's running in the Cup and realise his potential. He also, one may be sure, for he missed nothing in racing, was aware of the machinations of Harkaway's owner.

Later in the season Ferguson had Harkaway in the Chesterfield Stakes for which he had kept him and in which he intended to have one of his mighty bets at a long price, believing or hoping that Harkaway's true prowess still remained largely unknown in England. But he reckoned without Lord George, for Harkaway's running and his real ability had not, as we have said, gone unnoticed by him. As soon as he saw him amongst the starters he stepped in and backed him. He never did anything by halves and the weight of his money slashed the price. Ferguson was left to pick up what he could at a price far shorter than he expected and he soon learnt who had caused him the loss of the odds and his money. Harkaway won, again with ease as indeed he won most of his races, but the loss of his market had touched off Ferguson's inflammatory temper. He strode over to the Jockey Club stand and there declared at the top of his voice for all to hear: 'I've got the Chesterfield Stakes, and I will get more, but, by God, the public must understand that Harkaway is my horse, to win money for me, and not for any damn fellow, either a lord, or a lord by courtesy and a thief by the curse of God!'

The enmity between the two men continued unabated. Ferguson, unforgiving, was a terrible thorn in Lord George's flesh. Whenever their paths crossed on the racecourse he was ready with rude epithets referring to Lord George, these being delivered at the top of his stentorian voice and echoing across the stands and enclosures. This barrage of bad language was usually prefixed by the phrase 'that fellow in the buttons', which everyone knew to refer to the dictator of the Turf.

Wishing heartily to rid himself and the Turf of the turbulent Irishman, Lord George conceived that the best way to do it was to buy Harkaway himself. He sent an emissary to Ferguson bearing with him an offer he could not conceive being refused. He received an answer not only refusing it but turning it down in such scathing and insulting tones that one contemporary scribe, learning of them, declared he would not dare to commit them to print.

Indeed all this time Ferguson was waiting for an opportunity to take his revenge on Lord George for stealing his market in the Chesterfield Stakes. A little later it came to him and he made the most of it.

Lord George had a colt, Grey Momus, one of the best he had ever owned, who had won for him the Two Thousand Guineas, the St Leger, the Ascot Gold Cup and many other good races. He regarded him as virtually unbeatable, and, bringing him to Cheltenham, backed him as if defeat was out of the question. When Lord George went into the market in circumstances such as these his betting was formidable indeed. He once said of a fellow nobleman who owned the St Leger winner, Don John, and had only a small bet on him: 'If I had such a horse as Don John, I would not have left the last card seller at Doncaster with a rag on his back.' In Grey Momus he had such a horse now or reckoned he had.

His liabilities if he lost were going to be enormous and Harkaway was in the field.

Ferguson stood by his champion and he too went in and backed him as if defeat was out of the question. Thus battle was joined. It was a field of good horses but Harkaway slammed them all, giving Ferguson one of his greatest triumphs made all the sweeter by his defeat of Grey Momus.

Lord George had lost a great deal of money. He was hit in the pocket but the worse disaster was to his pride for Ferguson was determined to rub salt into the wound. He stood by his winner and, looking over to where Lord George was surveying his defeated runner and conferring with his jockey, shouted: 'That fellow with the buttons knows me now and he won't like spancelling the kicking Irishman I think.'

If, as we are told, Bentinck counted the thousands he had won as a general counted his prisoners after a victory, when Ferguson had finished with him after that Cheltenham race, he could only contemplate the thousands he had lost as a general counts his casualties after a rout.

The blow to Lord George's prestige was at the hands of Robert Ribsdale, another of his *bêtes noires*. Ribsdale came from humble beginnings, having started life as a boy in a livery stable. These lowly origins were in themselves sufficient to earn him Lord George's contempt, but Ribsdale prospered. He left the livery stable to become a groom in a series of great houses where he picked up manners, some polish and a great deal of inside information which his fertile brain put to good use. Soon he was able to set himself up as a professional gambler. Success came quickly so that within a short space of time he had an establishment of his own, rivalling some of those great houses in which he had served. Not only did he have in

28

'That fellow with the buttons knows me now and he won't like spancelling the kicking Irishman I think.'

his own stud and stable over a hundred horses for racing and breeding but he kept a string of hunters, the living best he could buy, which he rode brilliantly to hounds; his table abounded with fine wines and food cooked to perfection by a French chef. In addition he had acquired culture from somewhere for his library was full of first editions and his reading was not confined to the sporting press.

But Ribsdale was a crook. He used his wealth not only to bribe jockeys but owners as well on a scale which made his name a byword. Nevertheless, these activities brought in more and more wealth to maintain and keep Merton, his Yorkshire stately home, running in the way his lifestyle required of it.

Ribsdale's most audacious coup was to win the Derby of 1832 with St Giles. Bred by himself at Merton, not only was St Giles widely suspected of being a four-year-old but to make assurance doubly sure Ribsdale had squared the jockeys of the other fancied horses to let him win. The cost to him was said to be £25,000 but it was well worth it. The third horse, Trustee, was also owned by him and the fourth, Margrave, whom many held had the beating of St Giles had he been off, was owned by Gully, the prizefighter, an associate of Ribsdale's, and was deliberately stopped in order to get long odds for the St Leger. This, too, was accomplished since Margrave started at 8–1 for the last classic and won it as he liked. The total take of the two confederates over these two races was set down by contemporaries as being in the region of £200,000. 'Ribsdale,' it was said, 'could have managed such bits of Turf business easily, being a perfect master of the art of racing roguery.'

Ribsdale and Gully, however, fell out over the division of the spoils. At a meet of hounds shortly afterwards an argument developed, Gully believed Ribsdale was accusing him of cheating, Gully's temper was never far from hand, he lost it and struck Ribsdale with his whip, knocking him from his horse. Ribsdale sued for assault and was awarded £500 but the verdict did him little good.

Certain unsavoury details had emerged at the hearing. Lord George's reforming broom was beginning to sweep clean.

Stopping jockeys and others were commencing to look over their shoulders at this Nemesis which was stalking them. Soon he was hot on Ribsdale's trail, with the result that Ribsdale's fortunes began to decline. He attempted to retrieve them with a huge bet on his colt Hornsea in the St Leger of 1835, but either his hand had lost its cunning or, more likely, the objects of his machinations were now more wary of him. The attempt to fix the race failed and Hornsea was beaten into second place by Queen of Trumps. Ribsdale could not settle. He owed £70,000. He sold up and the great string of horses, the library, silver, plate, pictures and other adornments of high living went under the hammer.

But even then Ribsdale had the courage for a final fling. At the sale of his horses and effects there was one miserable under-sized yearling no one would look at. Divining its promise somewhere, Ribsdale retained it and arranged for his brother William to train it. Named Bloomsbury, he was entered for the 1839 Derby and won it.

But tongues wagged after the race. It was said that Bloomsbury was not Bloomsbury at all but another horse, a four-year-old, substituted for him and certainly the winner bore little resemblance to the wretched object retained from the sale. It was also said that Ribsdale had fixed Wrenn, the rider of the second, Deception, to stop him and Deception, in fact, came out two days later to win the Oaks as she liked.

These rumours, as was inevitable, came to the ears of Lord George and he took instant action. First he went to Mr Fulmer Craven, the owner of Deception and persuaded him to lodge an objection to the winner on the grounds that its entry contained a misdescription. The stewards called Ribsdale before them, examined him, and then issued a statement saying that Bloomsbury was qualified to start in the Derby and that the owner was entitled to the stake.

This setback did not deter Lord George. Once he got his teeth into something he would pursue it to the bitter end – and beyond. He next succeeded in persuading Mr Craven to take the matter to law and to serve notice on Weatherby's as stake-

31

holders, to withhold payment of the stake until the matter had been determined. The case was heard at Liverpool Assizes and a decision given in Ribsdale's favour. Lord George had lost again. Squire Osbaldeston, no lover of Lord George, expressed the almost universal feeling amongst racing people when he growled : 'His lordship did not get much praise for this proceeding.'

But, despite his victory, this minor disaster for Lord George turned out to be a major one for Ribsdale. The rumours about Bloomsbury's switching persisted; the costs of the enquiry and lawsuit took much of his owner's winnings. He was not getting any younger, his nerve was not what it was and the world was changing. His house and lands at Merton had already gone, there were no resources to fall back on; he was finished.

Even then Ribsdale could not keep away from horses and racing. He haunted Newmarket Heath, a lonely, impoverished and embittered old man. One morning he was found in a hayloft, dead. All that was left of the vast fortune he had once won on the Turf was three ha'pence in a trouser pocket.

2   Tribulations
of a Journalist
and of a Trainer too

The Derby of 1869 initiated a series of events which were to culminate in disaster for an outspoken, eccentric, often wrong-headed but always honourable sporting journalist.

Sir Joseph Hawley was one of the great racing magnates of the day. He came from an old established Kentish family; he had inherited wealth and standing; his colours, cherry and black, were carried to success in a series of great races to earn him the sobriquet of 'the lucky baronet'.

Sir Joseph did not run his horses for the public, he ran them for themselves and himself and, as his trainer, the great John Porter, said of him: 'He greatly resented the interference of other people with his racing projects.' This, amongst other things was to bring about the disaster that was to follow for, when that interference occurred, or he thought it did, he was ruthless in taking steps to counter it, regardless of what effect those steps might have on the market or, indeed, on his own image with the public.

In that year, 1869, there came the scratching of two of his horses, both of whom figured prominently in the ante-post market and which, to say the least of it, did not enhance his popularity with the public. Early in the season he and Porter had tried his colt, Vagabond, a pretty good certainty, they thought, for the City and Suburban. The news of that trial, however, got out, and when Sir Joseph sent his commissioner to back Vagabond he found him installed as favourite. Immediately he instructed Porter to take the colt out of the race and run him in the Great Metropolitan instead. The distance of the Great Metropolitan was too short for him and, despite being again made favourite by the betting public, he failed to gain a place. The baronet's popularity was not enhanced by this scratching and there was considerable critical comment.

Sir Joseph could also be impulsive and act too hastily as the action he took after that year's Derby was amply to demonstrate. In Pero Gomez, Sir Joseph and Porter had a very fancied colt for that Derby. He was, however, to their great disappointment, beaten into second place by Pretender, ridden by John Osborne. It was a muddling sort of race and Pero Gomez was badly interfered with at Tattenham Corner, being almost on the ground and coming in with mud on his nose. The verdict, however, only gave the race to Pretender by a head and both Sir Joseph and Porter thought their jockey, Wells, had ridden a bad race and blamed him for their defeat. Wells, in fact, believed that he had won; he took Pero Gomez into the winner's enclosure and was aghast when he heard the result.

Sir Joseph, who was in the habit of plunging when he fancied one of his runners, lost a great deal of money in that defeat. Disappointment coupled with disenchantment with Wells's riding, must have been the motives which impelled him to take the step he did on the day following the race. Rumours, perhaps put about by others suffering in their pockets and talking through them, were circulating that Mr Sadler, the owner of Pretender, had died on the morning of the race thus making his nomination void and his winner liable to disqualification. Sir Joseph, to his lasting discredit and without taking the advice of Porter, heeded these rumours, gave credence to them and sent the following letter to Messrs Weatherby, the stakeholders:

> Having heard a rumour that Mr Sadler, the nominator of Pretender for the Derby, died before the race was run, I give notice to you not to pay over the stakes until the matter is cleared up.
>
> (Signed) JOSEPH HAWLEY

. . . Pero Gomez was badly interfered with at Tattenham Corner, being almost on the ground and coming in with mud on his nose.

In fact, as a most cursory check would have revealed, Mr Sadler was not only alive and well but had been at Epsom to see his horse win. Porter's comment that this hasty action brought upon Sir Joseph 'no little odium' was a considerable under-statement, nor did it escape caustic comment from one Dr Shorthouse, the founder, owner and editor of a racing journal, *The Sporting Times*.

Carrying at its masthead the legend: 'High Toryism, High Churchism, High Farming and old Port forever', *The Sporting Times* was, as *The Pink 'Un*, to obtain lasting fame and noto-riety under John Corlett who was then on its staff and who softened its impact and broadened its base, but at that time it was under the sole control of its proprietor. Dr Shorthouse was no respecter of persons. He believed in hard-hitting journalism and acted on his beliefs. In character he was, as Porter records, 'a curious mixture of light-hearted geniality and Cobbett-like aggressiveness.' He was also a fearless exposer of what he thought to be sharp practices and irregularities from whatever quarter they sprang. It was he who tracked down and exposed the fraudulent machinations of a clever swindling tipster called W. H. Walter. When Walter threatened to sue if he did not receive a 'sufficient and abject apology', Shorthouse printed instead the splendid reply: 'We tell Mr Walter frankly and most decisively that he will get no apology from us. He may take his case to any court he pleases, criminal or civil – and the former is delicately hinted at – and we shall be happy to meet him there.' No proceedings followed and Walter, after a series of further frauds, was ultimately sentenced to twenty years imprisonment for forgery.

No adverse comment from Dr Shorthouse or anyone else could be made on Pero Gomez's subsequent running, for he took his revenge on Pretender in the St Leger and two days later beat him again over the same distance at the Doncaster Cup. There is little doubt, however, that the earlier events had placed Sir Joseph firmly in Dr Shorthouse's sights, and very soon another scratching by the baronet gave rise to what was almost a public outcry.

Sir Joseph had three horses in the Liverpool Autumn Cup, Blue Gown, winner of the previous year's Derby, Siderolite, and Lictor. There was an ante-post market on this race in which Blue Gown was made favourite with Siderolite also coming in for strong support. Shortly before the race, Sir Joseph, deciding that both Blue Gown's and Siderolite's trials had not been satisfactory, struck them out without notice or explanation to anybody. His third horse, Lictor, unconsidered in the betting but carrying £500 of Sir Joseph's money, came home a winner with the new favourite, Sir Lopez, only third. It was a result which did not please either press or public.

At the time these events were taking place, Dr Shorthouse, unfortunately for him, was ill and unable to supervise the editing and production of his paper. During the preceding months circulation had been falling off and at the weekly editorial meeting those left in charge conferred together to see what could be done to halt the decline. The remedy decided upon was to be a series of trenchant attacks on prominent racing personalities. In view of his recent actions – the ill-judged objection to the paying over of the Derby stakes and the two scratchings – it was perhaps natural that the first choice for these attacks should be Sir Joseph Hawley.

The task of writing the article was given to a young freelance journalist, Alfred Geary, who was only an occasional contributor since his main employment was as a traveller to a firm of wine merchants. Geary was a mild enough young man but once he had a pen in his hand it ran away with him and dripped vitriol. Given the commission he sat down and produced a most vituperative and vicious libel.

The article ran to thousands of words, almost every sentence containing an actionable calumny. It commenced by castigating the baronet as 'Sir Joseph Scratchawley', continuing in the same vein and becoming worse as it went on. It is obviously too long to reproduce here but one or two of its gems may be quoted to give the tenor of the whole:

Geary was a mild enough young man but once he had a pen in his hand it ran away with him and dripped vitriol.

What then can be said for the spoilt darling of the Turf, the little Jack Horner of the racing world, who has not only put in his thumb and pulled out one plum, but had had a whole grocer's shop of plums fall to his share, and yet tries all he can to bespatter his ancient name, before, in the course of nature, he is compelled to resign his seat in the Jockey Club, and his place in the Stewards' Stand to a better man. . . . Vagabond is tried, a moral for one on the early spring handi-caps, and has the pen put through his name, when every-thing has been got out of him that can be picked up in the market. It is reserved till the Liverpool Cup to place the coping stone on these coping proceedings. . . . The bloody hand on his escutcheon is emblematic of the victims who have fallen not in actual strife, but from the stab of the stable commissioner, and it will be many a long year before even the spurious popularity he once enjoyed will be restored to him. . . .

When Dr Shorthouse on his sickbed saw the article in print he was appalled. Immediately he wrote to Sir Joseph tendering an apology and in the next issue of the paper published the most abject recantation and withdrawal. Sir Joseph was not appeased. By the time the letter was delivered and the paper containing the apology had appeared he had consulted George Lewis, the celebrated Victorian high society solicitor, and had been advised to sue.

It is possible that Dr Shorthouse could have sheltered behind his contributor and also pleaded his innocence in the whole affair having been absent from the control of the paper through illness. Most honourably he refused to do either of these things and accepted full responsibility. It is said that in authorising publication of the offending article those in charge appreciated the likelihood of civil proceedings for libel in which they would be mulcted in damages but believed these would be offset by the increase in circulation it would bring – a course of action sometimes also pursued by later newspaper proprietors. They were therefore dumbfounded when they learnt that Mr Lewis was proposing to institute a prosecution for criminal libel, a comparatively new offence which they had not taken into account and which, if successful, would bring with it a prison sentence.

Certain of his friends then suggested to Sir Joseph that he might stay his hand in view of the fact that Dr Shorthouse was clearly innocent of criminal intent. He remained implacable and any doubts he might have had as to the correctness of the course he was taking were dispelled by the fact that Dr Shorthouse, who could be just as hasty and wrong-headed as himself, either wrote or at least passed for publication in his paper a paragraph hinting at unsavoury revelations affecting Sir Joseph which would come out at the trial.

The case was heard at the Central Criminal Court on 15 December 1869. Mr Serjeant Ballantine led for the prosecution; Dr Shorthouse conducted his own defence, once again, as one commentator remarked, proving the truth of the old adage that a man who is his own lawyer has a fool for a client. He was fined fifty pounds and sentenced to three months imprisonment in Holloway Gaol.

There was a considerable amount of public sympathy for the unfortunate doctor who had refused to name the author of the libel at the hearing. He was treated with respect and consideration in the prison which had earned the name of 'Happy Holloway' for the laxity with which regulations were applied to minor offenders of which Dr Shorthouse was considered to be one. His friends took advantage of this and were permitted to provide him with champagne and such delicacies as larks in aspic and plovers' eggs to soften the rigours of his stay. Moreover, a blind eye was turned to their assisting him in the consumption of these goodies at 'festive parties' held in his cell which was also provided with certain home comforts.

Again, however, Dr Shorthouse's paper proved a false friend. Glowing accounts appeared in it of how his friends were rallying round to help and the pleasant hours they passed with him in his cell. These came to the attention of a certain Mr Willes, a racing reporter on the *Morning Post* who wrote under

40

. . . a blind eye was turned to their assisting him in the consumption of these
goodies at 'festive parties' held in his cell . . .

the name of 'Argus'. Mr Willes had suffered from time to time under Dr Shorthouse's winged words. He was of a vindictive frame of mind and had not forgotten these attacks. He addressed a letter to the authorities complaining about the 'orgies' as he saw fit to term them, in Dr Shorthouse's cell and, when action on his complaint appeared to be ignored, threatened to bring the matter to public notice. Since he possessed a pen every bit as vitriolic as the doctor's, the complaint could not be overlooked. The governor of Holloway was instructed forthwith to cancel all privileges and to apply strict prison diet and regulations to this convicted criminal. For the remainder of his sentence Dr Shorthouse was restricted to prison diet and his visitors confined to regulation hours.

'The whole experience,' Sir George Chetwynd, a leading racing man of the time and a friend of the doctor's, wrote, 'if it did not kill him, materially shortened his life.'

James Drislane, known to all the racing world as 'Paddy', was an Irishman who trained in the North of England during the latter half of the nineteenth century. Like many of his race he had the gift of phrase and one of the stories he was fond of retelling concerned the catalogue of disasters that befell him within forty-eight hours when he brought two runners to the Northumberland Plate Meeting at Newcastle in the seventies.

Drislane, who had worked his way up from stable boy to head lad before launching out on his own, was up to every trick in the trade. He was especially adept at devising schemes to confound the touts who then plagued the training centres of the north. He was believed to have held a steeplechase trial by moonlight to the intense peril of his schooling jockeys and on another occasion smeared cow-dung, suitably diluted, on a fancied horse's quarters and second thighs to make it appear he was scouring. He then had him produced before the touts at walking exercise only. As soon as he knew the news that the horse was ill and had been stopped in his work had been flashed to the layers, he tried him in secret, got his price and won – the Chester Cup.

At this Newcastle Meeting he believed that he had again succeeded in keeping his intentions secret. In a race preceding the Plate he had entered a horse which he determined should not win, and to this end had put up an unknown boy from his yard. His instructions to the boy were that he was to make it appear he was out of control, to run so wide at the turn that anyone watching would realise it was useless to continue and then to pull the horse up, thereby securing for Paddy a good price the next time he ran. Unfortunately for him things didn't turn out that way.

The boy followed the first part of his instructions only too well. He was really and truly out of control and did run wide at the turn. But then the horse took such a strong hold that he was totally unable to pull him up; he ran on, came through his field and won.

When he dismounted, the boy, confronted with a raging and furious Drislane, burst into tears. 'Laugh, ye little devil, laugh, can't ye,' Drislane growled at him. 'Now is the time for ye to look plazed. Ye'll cry hard enough when I get ye alone to-night!'

This was a bad start to the day and worse was to follow. Drislane had backed his mare in the Plate to win him £1,000. She was only a little bit of a thing, the ground was soft and immediately before the race a heavy rainstorm came down. Seeing her in the parade ring with the rain pouring off her and observing her general air of dejection Drislane decided she had no chance in the conditions. He went off and hedged every penny of his bet. She won in a canter. 'Pon my word there's my luck again', Drislane declared, having won two races without a shilling on either winner. He then went off to deal out retribution to the stable boy.

Next morning, after seeing the horses and the boy, suitably

. . . he picked up the terrified monkey and hurled it at the organ-grinder.

chastened, on to the train at Newcastle Station he went into the town intending to buy a present for his wife. Putting his hand into his pocket he found that someone had been there before him, a pickpocket had done his work and his purse was gone. He was staring into the jeweller's window once more cursing his luck and wondering what he should do next when he became aware that an Italian organ-grinder with a monkey was operating immediately behind him. He was in the act of turning to get a better look at them when the monkey, who had been hopping about to the music, gave a sudden leap and landed on Drislane's shoulder. Sent off balance by the impact, Drislane stumbled and then went headlong through the plate glass window taking the monkey with him.

Added to his previous disasters this was all too much for the Irishman's temper. Cut about the face and hands and with his clothes in ribbons, he picked up the terrified monkey and hurled it at the organ-grinder. Then, bellowing imprecations, he got to his feet, charged out of the shop and began to belabour the unfortunate man with his stick.

Drawn to the rumpus a crowd gathered and a policeman appeared. Shouting his anguish to the skies in his native tones the organ-grinder remembered enough of his acquired English to lay a complaint with the policeman, charging Drislane with assault and battery. Then the jeweller came on the scene and announced he was claiming damages from Drislane for his broken window and loss of his valuable stock which had been scattered by the intrusion. Encouraged by this the organ-grinder promptly added that he, too, would claim damages for personal injuries to himself and his monkey. 'There's my luck again', Drislane declared dismally as the policeman produced his notebook.

The cases duly came off and Drislane had to pay up a considerable sum. 'Pon my word,' he would say when recounting the events. 'That Newcastle meeting was a great one for me!'

3 A Great old Gent and some other Gentlemen

Sir John Astley, or 'the Mate' as he was familiarly called, was a rumbustious old cove with a ready wit and a gift for repartee. Never at a loss for a ready quip, on one occasion when racing he was approached by a lady of generous proportions well outlined beneath a diaphanous dress. A new form book entitled 'Form at a Glance' had just been published and he was perusing it. Looking up at the lady he observed, 'Ah, form at a glance, I presume!' Although a baronet and a member of the Jockey Club, Sir John was perennially short of money and would have been the first to admit that he lived by his wits. A small private income barely sufficed to cover the most essential expenses for his wife and family – such as two fully staffed houses, one in the country, one in London and a stable of hunters and racehorses – and he had to make his racing pay. So when he went into the ring with his betting boots on the layers knew all about it and feared him. In the year in which the events about to be recorded took place he won no less than sixty-four races, £16,800 in bets and £15,871 in stakes and was yet, as he wrote after making up his book, 'cruel hard up'.

The reason for all this had much to do with the peculiarities of a horse called Peter and the brilliance of Fred Archer, the greatest jockey of his day.

Sir John had had his eye on Peter for some time. Peter, as has been said, had his peculiarities. He could be mulish, he was inclined to stop both at the start and through a race and all in all needed tender riding by someone who knew him. Given that, he was, in Sir John's own words, 'the best horse of his day or any other day', which is pitching it a bit high but then Sir

John delighted in superlatives and drama and all his geese were swans. He had been given first refusal of Peter at six thousand guineas which he had not got. However, when he had taken £1,000 to £60 three times on his own mare, Windsor, in the Chester Cup and she had come home a winner he wired Peter's owner his acceptance. Even then, after settling, he was still short of the full amount and had had to borrow £2,500 from a friend to make it up.

Archer was one of the few jockeys who knew Peter well and could get the best out of him. Archer was on friendly terms with all the great ones of his day, and, learning of the purchase from Sir John in conversation a little later, he, in Sir John's words, 'opened his eyes wide'. The reason for this was that Archer knew that Sir John had Charles Wood retained as his stable jockey and that Peter and Wood did not get on together.

Sir John, however, was full of his new purchase. His enthusiasm was increased when he watched a gallop in the Lime-kilns at Newmarket in which Peter gave a very good American horse, Foxhall, 2st 7lb and slammed him. There and then Sir John decided that the Manchester Cup over one and three-quarter miles was at his mercy and backed him accordingly. In fact, as he told the Honourable George Lambton, he had backed him to win a sum that would make him secure financially, adding, typically, 'at least for the moment', since money went through his hands like quicksilver.

So matters stood until a week before the race when Archer, who never gave up the chance of a winning ride and who knew Peter better than anyone else, as he was going out the gate at Kempton, handed Sir John a note saying: 'This will interest you, Sir John. I will ride Peter for you at Manchester if you wish.'

The note was from Captain Machell, a leading trainer of the day, telling Archer that if he rode his horse, Valour, in the Manchester Cup, he would run him, if not he would take him out. 'What answer shall I give the Captain?' Archer asked Sir John on his return.

Sir John would not budge from one of the unwritten laws of

racing, that an owner should never stand down (in modern parlance 'jock off') a stable jockey 'if he is a good rider and has
served him well and faithfully'. He told Archer in no uncertain
terms that he would not take Wood off the horse, adding in his
bluff over-confident way, but most unwisely: 'What chance,
anyway, has Valour, a non-stayer, to beat Peter there at a difference of four pounds in the weights?'

'It's a pity,' Archer told a friend. 'Sir John wants a turn
very badly and I'm afraid he won't get it now. You know Peter
won't go for Wood. I shall ride Valour for the Captain and he is
very dangerous on that course.'

He might have added, as Sir John knew well and it caused
him many moments of anxiety despite his confident predic-
tions, that he, too, was very dangerous on that or any other
course. For he was a genius. By a mixture of strength, superb
horsemanship and judgement of pace he could and did win
races on horses which had on the book no apparent chance at
all. And that was what happened here.

As a non-stayer Valour was freely quoted at 25–1. But
Archer, as always, had thought his race through. He decided to
bluff the other jockeys. From flag fall he set a strong gallop,
establishing an early lead and thereafter gave a marvellous
exhibition of waiting or perhaps dawdling in front. For
the other jockeys, thinking he was bound to come back to
them, let him go. Instead he had made up enough ground
to give himself time to rest Valour in front, thus saving
the non-stayer's strength and allowing himself to ride two
races as it were.

Peter, meanwhile, was not exerting himself unduly for
Wood. However, in the straight Wood had driven him clear of
the pack to challenge Archer. But he could not quite cajole him
to really run on. Despite the fact that Valour's reserves were
rapidly dwindling, Archer's tactics and strength saw him
through.

Sir John's own rueful words tell the rest of the story : 'Well,'
Sir John wrote long afterwards. 'It came to pass that my doing
the right thing was the cause of great disaster to me for in the

race Valour beat Peter a neck, which made a difference to me of over twelve thousand pounds.'

Modern owners, as many instances show, have not shared his scruples in their pursuit of prestige and prize money and it is sad to relate that his honourable gesture did Sir John little good for that defeat heralded a decline in his fortunes on the Turf.

'What is a gentleman rider?' is a question which has perplexed many since the inception of steeplechasing. Adam Lindsay Gordon, in his famous poem, 'How We Beat The Favourite', makes the groom ask his master a similar question about the rider of his chief opponent: 'A gentleman rider, well, I'm an outsider but if he's a gent, who the mischief's a jock?' Another versifier attempted to answer the question:

> The only reward that his honesty craves
>   Is a hardly contested success,
> No claim 'for expenses' his spirit enslaves
>   Sufficient is glory's caress.

Unfortunately for one hard-hitting journalist this 'claim for expenses' and its interpretation at the Baden Baden Autumn Meeting of 1862 was to lead to a duel and a death.

Baden Baden during the sixties and seventies of the last century and for some years afterwards was a high society rendezvous attended by the cream of the English 'gentlemen riders' who came not only for the racing but for the high jinks and high living and the pretty, available ladies of the chorus and the *demi-monde*. 'I'm off to Baden Baden,' warbled one of these with a taste for rhyming, 'where houris await, the favourite guest of Benazet the great, to folks spoiled like me your

Newmarket's a bore! So I've made up my mind to be seen there no more. Newmarket no more!'

At the autumn meeting the Gentlemen Riders' Hurdle Race was one of the chief events on the card and its winning carried with it considerable prestige. One of those most anxious to win it was Ludovic, Duc de Gramont Caderousse. Said to be the richest nobleman in France, personal friend of the Prince of Wales, protector of some of the most beautiful and alluring of the *grandes horizontales*, gambler, spendthrift and roué, known to some as the French Marquis of Hastings, de Gramont Caderousse was also the acknowledged leader of the select fraternity of French gentlemen riders.

In the year 1862, de Gramont Caderousse was at the height of his spectacular career. A duchess and an ambassadress had indulged in a public row on the racecourse over the bestowing of his favours and had become the talk of Paris; he had survived two duels, one of which the preceding year, with an Englishman, a Mr Harrison whom he had insulted, had left him with wounds in his side and arm which temporarily curtailed his racing activities; and he had lost a fortune at baccarat having to pay off his chief creditor with the grant of an annuity. His most extravagant exploit was to present his *maîtresse en titre* with a vast Easter egg left at her stage door. When opened, the egg revealed inside a carriage and pair together with attendants ready and waiting to convey her to his residence. On the racecourse his achievements were scarcely commensurate with his successes both social and scandalous. The only sort of record he could claim was that one of his horses, Trente et Quarante, ridden by himself, ran seventeen times and was only placed once.

Not everyone looked on the Duc's goings on with unjaundiced eyes. One of his most outspoken critics was a young English journalist called Dillon. The son of a parson, Dillon had spent most of his life in France and was then a racing reporter on the Paris paper *Le Sport*. Dillon did not think much of either the abilities or the snobbish exclusiveness of the French gentlemen riders and said so freely in his column. As

50

When opened, the egg revealed inside a carriage and pair together with attendants ready and waiting to convey her to his residence.

their leader de Gramont Caderousse was singled out for many of his attacks. The tenor of most of these was that if the Duc spent less time in bed with his mistresses or at the baccarat table and more in the saddle he would be better fitted to claim the title of a leading gentleman rider. These were picked up and echoed by the English contingent, one of whom remarked that 'to a French gentleman rider an actress is as necessary an appendage as a portmanteau'. It did not lead to any great *entente cordiale* between the gentlemen of the two nations.

Amongst the Englishmen assembled at Baden Baden for the big amateur hurdle was a Mr Thomas Pickernell who rode under the *nom de course* of 'Mr Thomas'. Tom Pickernell had had a chequered career, and his pretensions to being an amateur pure and unsullied were flimsy in the extreme. Shipped off at an early age to Tasmania 'to learn sheep farming' which is Victoriana for being kicked out, he had there started his racing career. Success came quickly for he was a superb rider; but even then his amateur qualifications had just as quickly become suspect. Soon he had been more or less requested to stop riding, turn professional or leave the country. Choosing the latter course he took a ship for home and, once arrived, started where he had left off. Already in 1862 he had won one Grand National on Anatis, and before his career ended he was to win two more. Although he had somehow managed to get himself elected to the exclusive Bilbury Club which in England gave him technical qualifications to call himself a 'gentleman rider' and ride as such, the suspicion that he pocketed both fees and expenses from unscrupulous owners remained uppermost in many minds. One writer using fictitious names expressed the prevalent view: 'It becomes no man to demand how Mr Smith became a member of the Dryberry Hunt . . . but it seems hard that I am compelled to admit that Mr Smith is a gentleman, when every antecedent of his life, and his associates, manners, and language, convince me he is not. . . .'

On this particular occasion 'Mr Thomas' had been brought over by a M. Pasquel to ride his Rigoletto in the big hurdle race. Since 'Mr Thomas' as when at home gave no indication of having independent means and since during his stay he appeared to prefer the company of jockeys rather than gentlemen and harlots to actresses and *demi-mondaines*, it was held by the French that he had no pretensions to appear in their company at all and it was also believed by them that M. Pasquel was paying all his expenses of the trip. Urged on by de Gramont, the Baden Baden stewards sat to consider the matter and called Pickernell before them. On his protesting that as a member of the Bilbury Club he had every right to ride, they allowed his qualifications to stand. This did not satisfy the French who, under the chairmanship of de Gramont Caderousse, held an informal indignation meeting on the balcony of the Stephanie Bains Hotel. Their protests availed them nothing though tempers were still running high when Pickernell went out to ride Rigoletto who was installed as the favourite at 5–4 on. They ran still higher when he won by half a length from the French Le Chatte ridden by Viscount Merlemont. The Duc de Gramont Caderousse was unplaced on his Duhallow.

On dismounting the Duc declared in the most cutting and contemptuous tones, loud enough for all to hear: 'Mistaire Pickernell is not entitled to rank as a gentleman in France.'

It was about as open and public an insult as could be imagined but the person at whom it was aimed took no notice of it though shortly afterwards he put about the totally untrue story that he 'landed the Duc a biff on the boko and knocked him head over heels!' This piece of fiction came when unpleasant stories of what actually happened were circulating. For Dillon, unfortunately for him, had been a witness to the whole scene. He most unwisely took up the cudgels on Pickernell's behalf writing an account of the whole affair entitled 'What is a Gentleman Rider?' This article, which received wide attention among the sporting fraternity, not only justified Pickernell but flayed de Gramont Caderousse and the whole corps of French gentlemen riders for unsportsmanlike conduct, bad horsemanship, being unable to take a beating and much more. Incensed, the Duc wrote a reply in which he referred to Dillon in such

. . . he was not an expert swordsman.

insulting terms that he was advised by his friends that he had no alternative in the code of honour then prevailing in France but to call the Duc out. Mistakenly, Dillon took this advice and issued the challenge which was accepted.

The weapons were épées and they met in a clearing in the forest of St Germain. Although de Gramont Caderousse had been out twice before he was not an expert swordsman. His skills however were sufficient to penetrate the clumsy guard of Dillon who had never handled any weapon in anger. After a few exchanges de Gramont ran Dillon through the chest. The journalist fell to the ground and died almost instantly, leaving the question 'What is a gentlemen rider?' unanswered, as it still is.

Captain E. R. 'Roddy' Owen was a dashing and engaging soldier rider during the eighties and nineties of the last century whose many qualities included reckless bravery and cool cheek. Once when reprimanded by a formidable general for taking too much time off from his military duties to go racing, with the words, 'I haven't seen much of you lately, Captain Owen', he blithely replied: 'My loss general, not yours!'

Owen lived for riding races – and winning them. Nick-named 'the headless horseman' because of his recklessness, charming and insouciant as he was off the racecourse on it he was a ruthless competitor. 'Try anything once' was his credo and he lived up to it. His success in doing so can be measured by the remark of one of his professional opponents that 'the Captain can get away with murder'. That, or something very like it, was what he nearly did in an incident-packed Grand National of 1891.

Owen's ride that year was on Cloister, later to become one of

Liverpool's immortals. Cloister then was at the beginning of his career, but, trained by Richard Marsh, he was quietly fancied by his trainer and his connections at the nice price of 20–1. Comeaway, ridden by Harry Beasley, than whom there has never been a better rider across Aintree or anywhere else for that matter, was favourite at 4–1, the whole of Ireland, it seemed, having crossed the Irish Sea to back him. Another fancied horse was Why Not, owned and ridden by a friend of Owen's, Charley Cunningham, whose ambition in life was to ride the winner of the National and that year saw what seemed to be his greatest chance of fulfilling it.

Coming to the last fence the three horses were in line. Comeaway on the outside, Cloister between horses and Why Not on the rails. At this stage Why Not appeared to be going by far the best of the three and looked all over a winner. He looked, in fact, to be going far too well for Captain Owen's peace of mind or his chances. There was all the room in the world at that wide last fence for the three of them but Owen was not disposed to give any of it to Cunningham. Cloister was a horse of immense power and strength as he was later to demonstrate over all the steeplechase courses in England. Using every bit of it Owen bore over and leant on Cunningham. Blinded and interfered with Why Not came down giving Cunningham injuries from which he nearly died and which ended his career in racing.

The fall left Comeaway and Cloister clear of the pack. Comeaway, who had suffered no interference at the last, went into a lead of several lengths. Owen set Cloister alight in hot pursuit.

It was as he closed the gap with Comeaway, half-way up the long run in that the 'headless horseman' lived up to his name. Fancying there was room on the rails between him and Comeaway twice he attempted to drive Cloister through it. No one ever succeeded in taking Harry Beasley's ground or making him yield an inch that was his. Each time Owen tried it Beasley closed the gap and shut him out. 'Harry', one racing reporter recorded, 'had the Captain in the same position as a man with a cork half-way in the neck of a bottle; one little push and it will go down.'

By the time Owen realised his mistake and that he was up against a rider as strong and ruthless as himself it was too late. He pulled out and came round. Although he cut down the lead, Comeaway held on to win by half a length. Had not he recklessly tried to take the inside Owen would probably have won by several lengths for Comeaway had broken down landing over the last and Beasley could not ride him right out. But Owen was not finished yet. He went into the weighing room and objected to Comeaway on the grounds of his rider 'having taken my ground on the run in!' When he came out and the objection became known he was very nearly lynched by the Irish contingent who were on Comeaway to a man. Let George Lambton, who was there, describe the scene: 'I can see him now, with his back to the wall, cool as a cucumber, saying, "All right, but wait till it's settled, then I'll fight every one of you, single-handed or the whole lot of you together!"'

He didn't have to. The objection was over-ruled but the 'headless horseman' was far from pacified. Muttering dire threats against Beasley he told Richard Marsh he would seek him out and give him a good thrashing. Marsh was far from pleased with him. He and those who had backed Cloister had seen their money thrown away along with the stake and the prestige of winning the great race. 'I shouldn't if I were you,' he told Owen. 'You might come off second best again!'

Beasley won that time all right. It was very seldom that he was caught napping but it did happen once in France. Most of Beasley's riding was done for Linde, the great Irish trainer, who on occasions could be as choleric as Tom Ferguson. Linde had a good chaser called Donny Carney, a useful sort but a difficult ride, whom he had sold to a Frenchman for £3,500 provided he won the Prix de Cascades in Paris. In this race he was opposed by only one other runner, Eau de Vie, who was trained by the same Richard Marsh who had been in charge of Cloister. Eau de Vie had good form for she had won the Sefton and Champion Chases at Liverpool, but in the Prix de Cascades she was set to give Donny Carney no less than 2st and neither Marsh nor Dan Thirlwell, his brother-in-law, a good amateur who was attached to his stable and was to ride her, thought she could do it. At these weights Linde and Beasley, too, thought the race a formality and Linde, who could put the money down and shake the ring when he wanted to, had a big bet.

Two fences from home it looked all over. Donny Carney was going so easily and Beasley appeared to have so much in hand that Thirlwell called across to him : 'Take your time, old chap. Make a race of it and let me down easily.'

Beasley, for once, was deceived and take things easily he did. At the last fence they were still together. Then, as they landed, Thirlwell, remembering Donny Carney's reputation for being difficult, set sail for home, getting the first run. True to form Donny Carney tried to stop. By the time Beasley got him going Thirlwell was several lengths to the good. Under his driving, and no one of that day and age could drive a horse with more strength than Beasley, Thirlwell was catching Eau de Vie fast but the post came just too soon, and he was beaten a short head.

The proposed purchaser refused to complete: Linde had lost the sale and his bet. His fury and wrath can be imagined. Even the French, who could not understand him, are said to have blanched and retreated from the unsaddling enclosure when his words erupted upon Beasley's head. Beasley's parentage, his abilities, his antecedents and character were explored in telling and lurid detail. Then, Marsh, who witnessed the encounter, records, for the first and last time in his life Linde went alone into the woods and wept !

There were two if not three schools of thought about George Abington Baird, the young Scots multi-millionaire who cut a swathe, sexually and otherwise, through the fringes of high society in the eighties. Some held he was an unmitigated blackguard; others that because of his origins – he was the son and grandson of Scots ironmasters who had fought their way up from penury to great wealth and his brief stays at Eton and Cambridge had failed to rub off all the rough edges – he was snubbed by the Establishment and by this driven into bad company to become the prey of spongers and touts who corrupted him; yet others agreed with George Lambton who seldom had a bad word to say of anyone, that he 'was a good judge of horses but a d...d bad one of men.'

It was his warning off in the year 1882 and in circumstances riddled with prejudice and prejudgement that embittered him, changed his character and set him on the path that led to dissipation and early death.

From the start Baird's ambition was to become a leading gentleman rider and to that end he put himself under the tuition of the great Fred Archer. Tall and stooped, he was of much the same build as Archer and like Archer he had to waste drastically to get down to a riding weight but in those early years he was dedicated to his task and he learnt fast. Soon he was a more than competent jockey winning races all over the place on the many horses which his income, said to be over £200,000 a year, enabled him to keep in a host of different stables. Once he was asked how many horses he had in training. 'Damned if I know' was the answer.

Thus he quickly came into prominence on the Turf as an owner and rider. The glamour conferred on him by his abilities coupled with his wealth and his lavish way of life soon, too, attracted the attention of many of the faster set of married women and those on the fringes of the *demi-monde* who made up the majority of the lady racegoers in those days. From the first he was sexually precocious and even when a very young man plundered the charms freely offered, discarding without a second thought each new conquest as soon as he tired of it or another, fresher one, was offered. The enemies amongst husbands and lovers whom he made as a result were legion and it boded ill for him that many were in positions of power and importance.

In 1882, the year in which he attained his majority, Baird was having considerable success both on the racecourse and in the boudoirs of the smart set. While under age he had assumed the *nom de course* of 'Mr Abington' in an attempt to conceal his racing activities from disapproving trustees and he kept this name to the end of his racing career though to his cronies he was universally known as 'the Squire'.

Amongst the horses that won for him that year was Billy Banks and it was on Billy Banks that his downfall occurred and disaster came to him. Billy Banks was entered in The Selling Hunters Flat Race Plate at the Fair Oaks Easter Park Meeting on 11 April and, opposed by only three other runners, duly went to post with his owner in the saddle.

One of the things about race riding which Baird had picked up from Archer was never to give away room or distance in a race. Archer was, in fact, at times both rough and ruthless towards his opponents whoever they were. But Archer was the leader of his profession and a law unto himself. He could do almost as he liked on the racecourse and in this respect at least was a dangerous man to copy. Nevertheless this was what Baird did since he, too, enjoyed a compulsive desire to win at almost any cost. In addition, therefore, to his predatory sexual activities which, as has been said, made him the object of a dangerous dislike by those in the seats of power, Baird became unpopular with his fellow riders through his roughness during a race and he had neither the personal charm nor the social position of one such as Roddy Owen who could employ equally ruthless methods and smile his way out of the consequences. Altogether, therefore, before that Fair Oaks Meeting, the fates were building up against Baird.

Despite there being only four runners, the Hunters Flat Race became something of a scrimmage which may or may not have been initiated by Baird. There was a deal of coming and going and bumping and boring. Bad language, of which Baird had a considerable flow at his command, flew about. At one point he threatened to put a fellow rider, who turned out to be the Earl of Harrington, over the rails if he didn't keep his bloody horse straight and get out of the way.

Baird and Billy Banks won the race by eight lengths, but for some reason Baird could not draw the weight and he was therefore disqualified on technical grounds. It was, apparently, a genuine mistake and no question of malpractice arose. Lord Harrington, however, returned to scale – he had finished last – seething with rage against Baird, furiously resenting the reflection on his riding abilities and the language addressed to him through the race by this young upstart. An exchange of hot words took place between the two of them in the weighing room during which Baird tendered Harrington a sort of apology but it was far from being a servile one and was, indeed, couched in such terms as to make, in the Earl's opinion, his offence all the greater. He thereupon stormed into the stewards' room and reported Baird for foul riding.

Two of the local stewards who heard the case had their knives ready and sharpened for Baird on account of his dalliance or worse with certain lights of love whom they regarded as their own particular property. They lost no time in deciding to 'send on' Baird to the senior stewards of the National Hunt Committee, since 'foul riding' if proved could carry with it the sentence of warning off the Turf which the senior stewards alone could sanction.

Baird's offence, in fact, was trivial. He had issued a threat but had not put it into action for Harrington finished the race unmolested and had not been either bounced against or put over the rails, but the senior stewards, too, knew all about

Despite there being only four runners, the Hunters Flat Race became
something of a scrimmage . . .

Baird's amatory exploits and his reputation of being too keen to win at all costs. It seems clear that they were only waiting an opportunity to teach this brash youngster a lesson. What evidence they heard and from whom, if indeed they heard any at all, has never been revealed but that he received a fair, impartial and unbiased hearing is to say the least of it unlikely. At any rate the stewards did not take long to make up their minds. The next issue of *The Racing Calendar* bore the stark notice: 'Mr Abington (Mr G. A. Baird) having been reported by the stewards of The Fair Oaks Park Easter Meeting for foul riding in the Hunters Selling Flat Race Plate, the Stewards of the Grand National Hunt Committee have decided that he be warned off every course where the Grand National Hunt Rules are in Force, for two years from this date. . . .'

It was a savage sentence for an offence – if it was an offence at all – that was committed every day on the racetracks all over England. No lives had been lost, no injuries caused, no damage done save the Earl of Harrington's ruffled feelings.

And that apology or what passed for it which set the seal on Harrington's fury and finally triggered off the complaint? Baird had looked down from his great height and said in that casual, insolent drawl perfected by his short stays at Eton and Cambridge. 'My mistake, my lord. I took you for a farmer!'

4　*A Pair of Rogues*

Reckless gambler – he once said if nothing else offered he would bet on two flies crawling up a wall – adventurer, amorist, journalist, racehorse owner and trainer, Bob Sievier was all of these and, his enemies would add, a lot more and worse besides. Before he was forty he had fought in a war, married into the aristocracy and been divorced, made a book in Australia, won and lost several fortunes and hit the headlines in sensational court cases. It was, however, the purchase, ownership, training and racing of the peerless filly, Sceptre, which was to bring about his greatest triumph and to end in personal disaster.

At the beginning of his fortieth year, 1900, Sievier appeared to be on top of the world. In Sceptre, his pride and joy, he had the prospective favourite for all five classic races which, with his natural panache and exuberance, he declared openly and loudly she would win and thus establish a record likely never to be surpassed. He had a country estate at Shrewton with a beautiful mistress installed there as hostess to preside over his lavish entertainments where champagne flowed like water and caviar was consumed by the case, and, for once, he had money in the bank.

It did not last long. In the spring he went to Monte Carlo, hit a losing streak, lost all he had and ran up enormous debts. To try to get it back he ran Sceptre in the Lincoln when she was not really ready and backed her to win him £40,000. She was beaten a head.

Despite her defeat Sceptre remained favourite for the Classics and when she won both the Guineas she was at such a short price for the Derby that the amount Sievier could get on would do little to aid his failing finances even if she won. By the time Derby Day came round he was in desperate need of cash and the duns were closing in. Somehow he managed to raise enough to back her to win him £33,000, though even this, were he to collect, would not see him out of trouble. His nerve or his courage were never in doubt and he refused to hedge a penny. But then ugly rumours began to circulate. It was whispered in the clubs and over the brandies and sodas beloved of Edwardian toffs that he was fielding against her and that he would have Sceptre stopped. It was all untrue but those who were ready to believe anything of him made much of it.

So, when she was beaten in the Derby disaster stared Sievier in the face. The rumours became a shout, the duns came crowding in. Somehow he staved them off and his nerve and his sense of humour remained intact. Playing billiards one evening he heard the marker call: 'Mr Smith receives six. Mr Sievier owes two.' 'Owes two, you fool,' Sievier shouted. 'I owe thousands!'

Unfortunately it was only too true and Sceptre's subsequent victories in the Oaks and the St Leger were at such short prices that they did little to help, nor did they do anything to still the rumours that he had had her stopped in the Derby, if anything, indeed, they gave them more credence and increased their circulation. He furiously resented them for his unblemished reputation on the Turf was the one thing he cherished above all else. But the flamboyance of his lifestyle which he refused to alter though duns hammered at his gates, did nothing to quell them. After Sceptre's St Leger victory he ordered fifty cases of champagne (for which he could not and did not pay) to be sent to Shrewton for the celebrations.

The end of the season saw him the winner of four of the five classic races, and heading the list of winning owners. It should have been a triumph, instead it was a disaster. His betting losses were such that he could not settle unless he sold Sceptre. He clung to her as long as he could but eventually in sadness he saw her sold, a testament to his folly though he would not

After Sceptre's St Leger victory he ordered fifty cases of champagne to be sent to Shrewton for the celebrations.

admit it. And those rumours about the defeat in the Derby still haunted his name and were eventually to bring about the crash.

Playing baccarat for high stakes during one Newmarket Meeting, Sievier won £7,000 from a Major Sellar. A day or so later after he had settled with Sievier in the Raleigh Club Sellar met Sir James Duke, a committee member. Duke knew Sievier and disliked him. He thereupon addressed Sellar and delivered himself of the following astonishing statement: 'You must know what character this man has. You know he was a murderer, a card-sharper and a thief ... I unmasked him before the stewards of the Jockey Club ... Sievier made money by Sceptre not winning the Derby ... You can tell all this to Bob Sievier with my compliments.'

Sellar did tell him and straightaway Sievier issued proceedings against Duke for slander. He cared little about his personal reputation but his good name on the racecourse meant everything to him. The real sting of the slander was in the accusation that he had had Sceptre stopped in the Derby.

The defence pleaded by Duke was a singularly cowardly one. He did not attempt to maintain the truth and accuracy of what he had said. Instead he pleaded that as a committee man he spoke the words on a privileged occasion and therefore they were not actionable. In addition he filed a plea in mitigation of damages which set out every questionable incident in Sievier's past (of which there had been not a few) so as to prove he was a person of such bad character that no words could adequately defame him.

The bad luck which had followed Sievier during that apparently successful year continued to pursue him for the case came on before Mr Justice Grantham and Mr Justice Grantham was a villain. He had obtained his position by a job, he was so prejudiced that some of his pronouncements from the bench bordered on the lunatic and he was a neighbour and personal friend of Sir James Duke.

It was unlikely that Sievier would receive justice from a tribunal presided over by such a man as Grantham and he didn't.

He did, however, score one victory and clear his name of the charge of having Sceptre stopped. Duke entirely withdrew this charge when asked by counsel : 'And it is your honest belief there was nothing wrong with it ?' [Sceptre's running]

'That is so', he said.

'You had heard rumours to the contrary ?'

'Yes.'

'Which you did not believe ?'

'That is so.'

Duke went on to say in terms which might have indicated to a less questionable tribunal a certain malice towards Sievier : 'I said however big a blackguard Sievier was I had always held the opinion that he would have given his ears to have won the Derby and so have his name enrolled amongst honourable men.' And at no time in the case were any of Sievier's actions on the Turf criticised or called into question.

But that was the extent of his success for Grantham saw that it went no further. He allowed every suggestion about Sievier's private life, however outrageous and unsubstantiated, to go before the jury, running the case flagrantly in Duke's favour, his supposedly impartial summing up being so biased as to be all but comic had its results not been so tragic. He commenced by telling the jury of Sievier: 'Now who is this man ? You must know, gentlemen, that he has been constantly in the company of gamblers, card-players, card-sharpers and the greatest scoundrels on earth. . . .' He continued in this vein becoming wilder and more fantastical as he progressed reaching the pinnacle of prejudice and fatuity when he referred to Sievier's cancelled presentation at Court, saying : 'Her Majesty would rather give up her throne than be addressed by such a man !'

It is hardly surprising after these and suchlike broadsides from the bench that the jury returned with a verdict of – one farthing damages.

At least the charge of stopping Sceptre had been disposed of in open court which mitigated the disaster but another, more terrible one was to follow.

No racing crime had been imputed to him either in the law

case or anywhere else nor had he ever been called before the stewards to explain the running of his horses. But he had enemies in the high places of racing arising out of his broken marriage and a youthful encounter in Australia with one of them. Certain members of the Jockey Club having scanned the evidence of Sievier's private life and listened to Grantham's summing up succeeded in passing a resolution authorising their solicitor to send a case to counsel to determine whether there was any means of ridding the Turf of Sievier.

The counsel chosen was none other than C. F. Gill who had acted for Duke in the slander action. He was not likely to be sympathetic to Sievier and on receipt of the case he dredged the authorities eventually coming up with a very doubtful forty-year-old precedent where a man called Atkins had been warned off after being convicted of fraudulently using loaded dice. Though it was far from being on all fours with *Sievier v Duke*, Gill advised that it could be followed. Pressed by the rump who hated Sievier the stewards took his advice. The next issue of the *Racing Calendar* bore the following notice: 'The Stewards of the Jockey Club have warned Mr Robert S. Sievier off Newmarket Heath.'

He had touched the heights, now he was in the depths. He had not been allowed to say one word in his own defence before the stewards; he had lost everything, his money, his beloved mare and, what mattered most of all, his unblemished career on the Turf, and all through an unjust judge and the malice of a few.

One of Sievier's chief enemies and he had many – was Chief Inspector Drew of Scotland Yard. Drew was much concerned with racing and of his reputation on and off the Turf it is perhaps sufficient to say that he had earned and was universally known by the sobriquet as 'Tricky' Drew. At that time off the course betting for cash was, of course, illegal, but equally, it was much carried on especially in public houses with the publican acting as bookmaker. It was widely believed that Drew was not above taking a solacium from the landlords of these houses for turning a blind eye on their activities.

On one occasion it was reported to him that a new publican was operating this sideline so he sent two of his plain clothes officers to investigate. By this time, however, Drew's activities and propensities were pretty well known throughout the East End. Having ordered and consumed several drinks the officers entered into conversation with the landlord presently bringing it round to racing. 'What odds are you offering on the Cambridgeshire?' one of them asked him.

'Ten to one bar two', was the answer.

'What two are you barring?' came the next question.

'You and your pal', was the reply.

If Drew had expected a soft touch there he was to be disappointed.

Horatio Bottomley's time on the Turf as an owner coincided to some extent with Sievier's. Bottomley was a financier, an MP, a floater of fraudulent companies, proprietor of a muck-raking paper, *John Bull*, a demagogue and a swindler. Like Sievier his private life was gaudy in the extreme, his tastes in women and wine flamboyant and extravagant. He kept a seraglio of mistresses, most of them drawn from the chorus line and installed in various London flats and hotels. Like Sievier, too, he had a taste for champagne. Pommery was his tipple. He breakfasted off kippers and a bottle; if there were no kippers then the bottle by itself sufficed. Another bottle followed in midmorning, there was much more at lunch, a further bottle instead of tea and, of course, a magnum to get through the evening. (Maurice Healy, in his charming account of his adventures with wine called *Stay Me with Flaggons* remarked of him [Bottomley] that 'the late Horatio Bottomley had many demerits, but he was clever enough to appreciate the value of a good draught of champagne at eleven o'clock in the morning'.)

On the racecourse his consumption of 'bubbly' was conspicuous even in that age of gargantuan appetites. Although he was an owner for many years and a gambler on a scale that rivalled and sometimes exceeded Sievier's he never really learned about horses and racing. Sievier despised him and referred to him as a 'fly-mug' which is as good a way of describing him as any.

Although he knew little about horses or the intricacies of racing, Bottomley's fertile brain did devise one ingenious and audacious scheme for defrauding the bookmakers. Bottomley's trainer, Batho, specialised in selling races, which by and large are the lowest form of racing. On Batho's advice Bottomley had bought a selling plater called MacMerry with which he ran up a series of successes in these races. When MacMerry was running Bottomley would don a special bowler which became known as his 'MacMerry hat' and the word would go round the ring that 'the old man has got his MacMerry hat on' as the layers made ready to accept his frequently outrageous bets.

It may have been MacMerry's successes which inspired Bottomley's undefeatable plan for making 'a stone cold racing certainty' out of betting on sellers.

He instructed Batho to watch the entries in selling races and report to him when there appeared to be a likelihood of only three or four runners. On receipt of this information he would go into action. This consisted of buying up the whole lot just before the race. It had to be done sparingly and with care for it required small fields, owners willing to part and co-operative jockeys, but it was done with success to the considerable enrichment of Mr Bottomley's coffers. On one occasion he actually engineered an objection which he knew would be overruled. Thus he was able to add a bet on the outcome of his objection to his other wagers. When the result was announced he was paid three times over. He had backed the winner and had a bet on the placing of the first three all of which he had, of course, previously arranged.

Stewards were less active in those days than now. 'Three blind mice' Sievier called them on one occasion which did not

. . . they became suspicious . . . when the horse Bottomley had arranged to win dropped dead on the way to the post . . .

enhance his popularity with the Establishment. 'They could hardly tear themselves away from the port decanter to watch the race', one of those in the know about Bottomley's little scheme said of them. At last, however, even they became suspicious and then disaster struck when the horse Bottomley had arranged to win dropped dead on the way to the post and the other jockeys found themselves without instructions as to a new finishing order. As this was just before it had been whispered in Bottomley's ear that the authorities were about to institute further enquiries into his activities in sellers, the fraud came to an abrupt end, but it had been good while it lasted.

Nemesis, too, caught up with Bottomley in time. His swindling with other people's money was ultimately exposed and he was sentenced to seven years penal servitude for fraudulent conversion of trust funds. Raising the cash to pay the bookmakers – he described settling on Monday mornings as going through the Garden of Gethsemane – was at least partly responsible for his putting his hand into this particular trust fund. When the crash came his stud was disposed of and twenty of his horses were sold for under £2,000, a woefully small return on all the thousands he had expended, but his interest in racing never left him. A friend, visiting him in prison, came on him cutting the Governor's lawn. He opened the conversation by saying to Bottomley, 'Still on the Turf I see.'

Whatever else one can say about those Edwardian rogues, Sievier and Bottomley, and one can say a lot, they had three redeeming features – nerve, courage and a sense of humour. Early in his incarceration Bottomley was in his cell stitching mailbags. A prison visitor passing by remarked to him: 'Ah, Bottomley, sewing?'

'No,' was Bottomley's answer. 'Reaping.'

5   Two Derbys

'He destroyed a marquis, avenged a commoner and attained Turf immortality.' These words were written about Hermit, the Derby winner of 1867 and the story behind them contained all the elements of scandal and romance beloved by the Victorians – an elopement, jealousy, rivalry on the Turf and the squandering of great fortunes 'on the health of a two-year-old or the fall of a card'.

Henry Chaplin, squire of Blankney Hall in Lincolnshire and twenty-five thousand broad acres had come into his inheritance at the age of twenty-one. He was one of the most popular and sought after young men in Victorian high society. A personal friend of the Prince of Wales, he entertained lavishly for him at Blankney. Everything he did was done with an open hand including hunting the Blankney Hounds at his own expense. 'Tall, fair and well-proportioned, the picture of health, he was indeed a handsome specimen of the Anglo-Saxon race', Lord Willoughby de Broke wrote of him adding : 'May we say no one was half such a country gentleman as Henry Chaplin looked ?' No wonder in later days he earned the title, 'El Magnifico'. Rich, affable and easy-going, at the age of twenty-four only one thing was lacking to him – a suitable wife to set off his splendours. But this too, appeared in prospect for he had secured the affections – as he thought – of Lady Florence Paget, 'The Pocket Venus', the reigning beauty of her day.

But Chaplin, though he did not know it, had a rival.

Henry Weysford Charles Plantagenet, fourth Marquis of Hastings, was two years younger than Chaplin though he too had been up at Oxford with him. Save in his early inheritance of great wealth and estates he was in every way the other's antithesis. A sickly child he grew up to be a weak and weedy man, defects which he attempted to cover by fast living in fashionable circles. Spoilt and cosseted from birth, brought up without a father's hand, surrounded by sycophants, he only lived to gratify his desires and to indulge in his passion for horses, racing and, more especially, gambling. He once declared that his greatest ambition in life was to 'break the ring' and on one or two occasions, with the vast wealth then at his disposal, he went very near to doing it. Success on the Turf came to him quickly and he capitalised on it by gambling in sensational amounts making him a figure to be pointed at in wonder whenever he set foot on a racecourse and gaining for him the notoriety he loved, since, in the slang of the day, a 'perfect cocker' was what he aimed to be. He trained himself, too, to suffer setbacks when they occurred without betraying a flicker of emotion and already certain of these setbacks were heavy enough to make inroads into even his vast fortune. Languid, feline, arrogant, wherever he went he carried about him an air of controlled recklessness which would make him either the darling or the damned of the gods and which fascinated many women of all classes.

But Hastings, too, lacked a wife and wanted one to enhance his image, to preside over his household and to complete his conquests of society, racing and the ring. He cast his eyes upon the most beautiful woman in England, 'The Pocket Venus' but she was pledged to another – his friend and acquaintance, Henry Chaplin.

Lady Florence Paget, was spoilt, wilful and self-centred. She loved excitement. Racehorses, racing and all the tinsel glamour of the racecourse, thrilled her. Chaplin's sporting interests were then centred on hounds and hunting which were too slow for her. Harry Hastings, 'the perfect cocker', who could win or lose a fortune on the shortest of short heads or the turn of a card without betraying a flicker of emotion, who was engaged in an exciting endeavour to break the ring and plung-

75

ing ever more heavily to attain it, attracted her far more and provided the excitement she craved.

But she did not tell Henry Chaplin any of this and the preparations for the marriage proceeded. The date was fixed for mid-July 1864. The wedding dress was delivered and she paraded in it before her father – and then she bolted.

During all this time she had been in secret communication with Hastings. Picking her up by arrangement in Oxford Street outside the entrance to Marshall and Snelgrove's emporium, he drove her in a hansom cab to St George's Hanover Square and there, by special licence, they were married.

Society was at first astounded and then scandalised. All the sympathy was with Chaplin. Hastings did not care. Winning The Pocket Venus in the way he had was another feather in his cap, another success against the odds. That was all she was really – a success symbol for the marriage went awry almost from the start. He had always had a taste for low life ; soon he was spending more and more time in the stews of London than at home. Never physically robust his consumption of brandy and raw spirits quickly began to undermine his frail constitution. Surtees used him as a model for Sir Harry Scattercash in *Mr Sponge's Sporting Tour* – 'A tall, wan, pale young man with a strong tendency to delirium tremens. That, and consumption, appeared to be running a match for his person', which was almost exactly a description of Hastings at that time. And, always, stupendous sums were being risked by him on his horses and at the gambling tables. Not all his racing bets were losing ones for he had, when sober, shrewd appreciation of the worth of his horses and the way of placing them. But vanity played too big a part in their making. He always had to be ahead of the ring and the ambition to break it was still raging within him and was to lead to his downfall, that and the personal enmity he conceived for Chaplin, the man he had wronged.

What, meanwhile, of Chaplin, the rejected suitor, the centre of the scandal which was reverberating through society ? At Blankney during morning prayers a special prayer was said 'for

Picking her up by arrangement in Oxford Street outside the entrance to Marshall and Snelgrove's emporium . . .

God to send him a comforter to help him forget how cruelly he had been wronged by a woman'. He took himself off to Scotland and deer-stalking and then went to India for a year, tiger shooting amongst the maharajahs, to try to forget.

But he did not forget. Although he was a magnanimous man, the instinct of rivalry or revenge must have played some part, perhaps subconsciously, in what he did next. On his return he plunged into frenzied activity on the Turf which, in its excesses, came near to matching Hastings. 'He is buying horses as if he was drunk and backing them as if he was mad', a relation wrote of him during this time.

At Mr Blenkiron's disposal sale, Chaplin's racing manager, Captain Machell, purchased on his behalf a colt by Newminster out of Seclusion afterwards named Hermit for a thousand guineas. Hastings was the underbidder and when he discovered who the purchaser was he was furious. Hastings' fortunes were by this time fading as fast as his health was deteriorating and his marriage breaking down. And, as often happens in such cases, it was the wrongdoer not the wronged who bore malice and nursed a grudge. Hastings' unstable mind laid the blame for his reverses on Henry Chaplin and then, to cap it all, finding that he had lost Hermit to him he coupled the colt with his owner in conceiving an irrational hatred for them both.

Hermit's two-year-old career showed such promise that he became one of the winter favourites for the Derby. Hastings, however, whose hatred for the colt and his owner now bordered on the manic, decided that Hermit could not win and that he would ruin Chaplin through his horse. He therefore commenced to lay against Hermit with every shilling he could find and many which he had borrowed from Padgwick, the moneylender. 'Harry is laying against Hermit as if he were already dead', The Pocket Venus wrote plaintively to a friend. He even went to the extent of striking bets with Chaplin himself to the tune of £20,000 that Hermit would not win and by the time the day of the race came round he stood to lose upwards of £120,000 if Chaplin's colt won. And, in the days leading up to the Derby at first it looked as if he was going to bring this wild gamble off.

In a rough gallop a week before the race Hermit stumbled, nearly fell and pulled up with blood streaming from his nostrils. He had broken a blood vessel. When the news was brought to him a disconsolate Chaplin wanted to scratch him at once. Both Captain Machell and Custance who had ridden the colt in his gallop, after a lengthy discussion dissuaded him saying that the injury might not recur and that Hermit should be allowed to take his chance. So, with only light work in the final week, the colt came to Epsom. There had been no recurrence of the 'breaking' and to all appearances he was fit and ready to run for his life. But the news had got out. He had drifted in the betting to 66–1 and his starting price was returned at 1000–15.

Chaplin, reassured by Machell, had now recovered his confidence. 'I told all my friends', he later recounted, 'that if Hermit was in the front rank as the horses came into sight at the top of the hill, I thought he would certainly win. No one, of course, believed me, and they thought me a fool.' Meeting Hastings as they left the parade ring, magnanimous as ever, he told him just that and advised him to cover his bets. 'Thank you, Henry, I shall not trouble', was the drawled and disdainful reply.

It was a miserable day and flurries of snow were blowing across the course at the start. There were no starting stalls or gates in those days. Inevitably the horses became fractious and there were no less than ten false starts before eventually they were sent away.

In the race Hermit was hardly seen at all until close to the finish. Then he came on with a run to challenge the leader, Marksman, who was being shouted home a winner. Hermit just caught him, stayed on a fraction better and won by a neck.

That neck cost Hastings all of £120,000 and what was left of his health. He settled his bets with the ring but some of his estates had to be sold to find the money and he went deeper and deeper into Padgwick's toils, moving Admiral Rous, the great

It was a miserable day . . . and there were no less than ten false starts before eventually they were sent away.

handicapper, to write a little later: 'What can the poor fly demand of the spider in whose web he is enveloped?' Moreover, he did not at once settle with Chaplin and had to beg for time which, again with great magnanimity, was given him but the humiliation must have been terrible.

He died a year later ravaged by Bright's disease, brought on by his excesses, worn out, broke, his lands and fortunes by then gone entirely to the ring and the moneylenders in wild betting to recoup his losses over that Derby. 'Hermit fairly broke my heart,' he declared in his dying days, and then, with a flash of that spirit which had made him long to be 'the regular Cocker': 'But I didn't show it, did I?'

The Derby of 1913 was probably the most sensational of all time, bringing not one but a whole series of disasters in its train.

Major Eustace Loder, a member of the Jockey Club, a steward at leading courses and a prominent breeder, had personal and family reasons for an antipathy to C. Bower Ismay, owner of the favourite, Craganour. Bower Ismay had bought Craganour when he was a 'cull' or throw-out from Loder's stud which, since Craganour developed into an exceptional racehorse, did nothing to lessen the antagonism between the two. The Ismay name was prominent before the public then and not happily either for his brother, Bruce Ismay, chairman of the White Star Line, had been blamed, quite unfairly, for saving himself at the expense of others when the *Titanic* went down the year before.

Major Loder was the senior of the Newmarket Stewards when Craganour was held to have been beaten a head in the Two Thousand Guineas in one of the most doubtful and controversial decisions ever given in a classic race. Virtually everyone who watched that finish believed the judge had made a mistake and that Craganour had won by at least a length. 'They've put his number up but they'll damn soon take it down', one trainer said to a friend. But they didn't, nor did the stewards call for any enquiry or take any action.

Craganour was ridden by Saxby who, oddly enough, was a protégé of Loder's. Robinson, Craganour's trainer, was a highly strung, opinionated and bad-tempered man. He was a terror to his stable lads and indeed to almost everyone with whom he came into contact. Jack Leach recounts how, when he came on to the Downs to work his string, he invariably held up his handkerchief to test the wind and, equally invariably, from whatever quarter it came, cursed it. One of the lads, greatly daring, observing day in, day out, said to him : 'Surely, Guv'nor, the wind can't always be from the wrong direction.' 'Yes it can,' came the growled reply. 'If it's in the north it's bad for the horses, and if it's in the south or west it's bad for my pigs. And if it's in the east it's bad for me.' He had a hut made for him on the Downs to which he would repair if the wind was in the east. The lads named it 'the Guv'nor's unrest'.

With such a temperament it was inevitable that Robinson should be critical of his jockeys and he was especially critical of Saxby's riding in that Guineas with the result that he was stood down or, in modern parlance, 'jocked off' for the Derby for which Craganour remained a firm favourite. This action, it need scarcely be said, pleased neither Saxby, who was bitterly resentful, nor Major Loder who felt that his protégé had been unfairly treated. Robinson wanted Danny Maher, the brilliant American, to ride Craganour but he was claimed elsewhere and in the end, after much toing and froing, the choice fell on Johnny Reiff another American then riding in France. This was a mistake for Reiff, though an outstanding rider, did not enjoy the best of reputations either on the Turf or off it for he was suspected by the authorities and disliked by many of his fellow jockeys. The other riders' sympathies were, in fact, all with Saxby for the treatment meted out to him and Reiff could look forward to being given a rough passage round Epsom, not that that was likely to worry him much for he was as tough as the leather in his riding boots and had already won two Derbys.

Saxby was given the ride on Louvois who was fancied by his stable. The French had a useful challenger in Nimbus ridden by George Stern another tough jockey who could hold his own in any company if it came to a rough passage and of whom a fellow jockey once said to John Corlett, then editor and proprietor of *The Pink 'Un*: 'Governor when you see George Stern riding at a meeting where there are no stewards, *back him.*'

There was also in the field Aboyeur, a 100–1 chance, a bad-tempered brute who could and would savage anything that came near him, human or equine, if the fancy took him. He very nearly did not run at all for he pulled up lame after his final gallop and it was only after much discussion and veterinary advice that he was allowed to take his chance. Even then he was equipped with blinkers to try to curb his savage propensities.

Altogether, as may be imagined, tension was running high everywhere before that Derby and, unknown to all, another factor had entered into the preliminaries which was to lead to a separate and unique disaster.

The suffragette agitation was then at its height and one of the most militant and fanatical was a young woman called Emily Davidson who had already served a term in prison for her activities. On the morning of the race she took two suffragette flags from their HQ, wove one around her waist, carried the other and made her way to Tattenham Corner.

So the stage was set with Loder the master of ceremonies as it were, for he was again the senior steward on the day. Ismay and Robinson were both on tenterhooks. They owned and trained the hottest Derby favourite for years since Craganour had been backed down to 6–4 against which, in itself, was enough to cause nervous strain. But that was not all they had to worry them for between the Guineas and the Derby both had received anonymous threatening letters and telephone calls,

The suffragette agitation was then at its height . . .

some from supporters of Saxby, others apparently connecting Ismay with his brother and the sinking of the *Titanic* which was still fresh in everyone's mind. Robinson, especially, with his temperament, was near to breaking under the strain.

At the post too there was more than the usual tension. Everyone knew of Saxby's resentment for he had not been slow or silent in expressing it. The English were eyeing the French riders and remembering some of the rough treatment handed out to them when they went to ride in France. The French were ready and waiting to hold their place and to give as good as they got if it came to a rough house.

And it did. It was probably the roughest Derby on record.

At Tattenham Corner, Aboyeur was in the lead. Craganour, closing on him, swerved and looked about to veer over on to him. Aboyeur, showing his true colours, promptly tried to savage him. Reiff 'put him back' and Aboyeur then went all over the place first hampering those on the rails and then leaning outwards on to Craganour. By this time a general fracas was taking place leading one of the French jockeys to describe it afterwards as the nearest thing to taking part in a bull fight. Craganour and Aboyeur passed the post locked together but Craganour had his head in front, and the judge pronounced him the winner.

The owner of Aboyeur, very wisely since in the opinion of most it was his colt which had caused all the trouble, said most emphatically that he would not object. The 'all right' was called and almost immediately cancelled for the stewards, at the instigation of Loder, decided for the first time in history that they themselves would object to the winner.

One might have thought that was sensation enough for one afternoon but immediately after the announcement news came in that Emily Davidson had thrown herself in front of the King's horse, Anmer, at Tattenham Corner, bringing him down, injuring his jockey and herself sustaining injuries from which she was unlikely to recover.

Loder conducted the enquiry. Only two stewards sat, himself and Lord Wolverton which was in itself highly irregular

since no proper quorum was therefore constituted. Lord Rose-
bery, the third steward on the day, had had a runner in the race
and thought it improper for him to sit. Loder, apparently, saw
no reason to co-opt another and since Lord Wolverton was a
nonentity, the conduct of the enquiry was left entirely to him.
Nor did he take long about it. The investigation of such a difficult and important finish in the premier race on the calendar
took only a brief fifteen minutes, Saxby being the chief witness. 'If', as one commentator wrote afterwards, 'the stewards
were looking to disqualify Craganour they were likely to get
from Saxby the evidence they were seeking.'

The vast majority of those present including the bookmakers who offered 5–1 against Aboyeur getting the race were of
the opinion that Craganour should keep it. They were wrong.
Loder's decision was that Craganour should be disqualified
and placed last and Aboyeur awarded the race.

Loder, the instigator of it all, can scarcely have anticipated
the storm which was about to burst over his head. The following day virtually every newspaper, sporting or otherwise, con-
demned his decision in no uncertain terms. Now it was his turn
to be subjected to a deluge of anonymous threats.

Disaster piled on disaster. Ismay appealed to the stewards of
the Jockey Club, but due to some mix-up the appeal was out of
time and the senior stewards declined to hear it. He then
applied for and got an interim injunction instructing the stakeholders to withhold the stake pending a high court action. In
the meantime a substantial offer for Craganour from the
Argentine came in. Disgusted with the whole thing he sold the
colt and dropped the action.

To complete the catalogue of disasters: Loder, already a
sick man suffering from Bright's disease, died a year later. The
verdict and subsequent furore broke Robinson's health and
he, too, only survived, a sick and ailing man, to die after a few
years in his early fifties. Her injuries proved fatal to Emily
Davidson and she died in hospital. Aboyeur never won another
race. He was sold cheaply to Russia – 'an appropriate place',
one who knew him well wrote of him then, 'for a savage bar-

barian of a horse who had brought about the downfall of an equine aristocrat' – disappeared in the Revolution and was never heard of again. And, to cap all these disasters was the sad tale of a member of the Stock Exchange. J. B. Booth, one of *The Pink 'Un* staff, dined with him that night and was told how he had drawn Aboyeur in the Calcutta Club sweepstake. Thinking it was worthless he gave the ticket to his office boy who had drawn £1,875!

The decision of the stewards to deprive Craganour of the race played havoc needless to say with the betting. One of its most disastrous results is related by Campbell Russell. An owner-trainer and amateur rider who liked to shake the ring and did so on occasions Russell advised wealthy men on their wagers and worked commissions for them. Before the commencement of the 1913 flat season he had a consultation with 'a well-known financier' who asked him to advise on a likely treble. If the treble came up it would yield a large sum and Campbell would share in the profit.

Having studied the form books and consulted his records and recollections, Campbell decided that Cuthbert would win the Lincoln, Drinmore the City and Suburban Handicap and Craganour the Derby. The sum they stood to win was over £100,000.

Cuthbert duly won the Lincoln narrowly beating Berrill-don. The friends were jubilant but their jubilation did not last long. An objection was lodged; and soon news came that it had been sustained and the race awarded to Berrilldon. That put an end to the treble.

Nothing daunted, the financier decided to back Drinmore for the City and Suburban and Craganour for the Derby in a £600 double which, if they came home, would net him

£50,000. Drinmore won the City and Suburban by the shortest of short heads. The financier suffered agonies of nerves waiting to see if a second objection would come. It did not and once more jubilation reigned, Campbell assuring his client that Craganour was a certainty for the Derby, that objections were unheard of in the Derby and in any event the lightning never struck in the same place twice.

What the financier went through for the third time can only be imagined. 'Craganour has done nothing wrong to cause his disqualification', Russell assured him. 'But', Campbell wrote long afterwards, 'he had in official eyes, and the scene as Robinson, Craganour's trainer, walked out of the winner's enclosure was the most painful remembrance I shall ever have of that tragedy next to that of my friend walking quickly away from the racecourse, where he vowed he would never tread again. And neither to Epsom nor any other course did he come. Cuthbert, Drinmor, Craganour! I fancy those names will be found written on his heart when he dies.'

6   *A Band of Brothers*

Siegfried Sassoon wrote of Frank and Harry Brown, two brothers prominent on the steeplechasing scene before and after the First World War, that they were: 'Desperately fine specimens of a genuine English traditional type which has become innocuous since the abolition of duelling.' It was an apt enough description even though on the racecourse they both, but especially Harry, could scarcely be described as innocuous.

Of the two, Harry was the more self-assertive, combatant and controversial. He gave a damn for nobody, least of all the authorities and many, including the majority of his fellow amateur riders, went in some fear of him. Such was the skill and strength in the saddle of both the brothers, however, that the services were in constant demand by owners and trainers. Harry Ussher, the leading Irish steeplechase rider during their heyday, was once asked who was the best amateur then riding in England. His reply was: 'Well, it depends on how you want them ridden. I would say Harry Brown is certainly the best at stopping them and his brother Frank may be the best when you want them to win.'

Stories gathered about Harry's name like flies on a fly-paper. He was even more successful than Frank and once headed the list of winning jockeys amateur and professional becoming champion of the year, a feat only once accomplished before. But he had his share of disaster, much of it brought about by his combative temperament and unguarded tongue. Once he terminated a heated row with a neighbour out shooting by declaring: 'All right, but I'll beat you a field in our point-to-point.'

His brother commented that no one, least of all himself, knew just how he hoped to do this since both would be riding their own hunters neither of which had the necessary speed to set up such a lead.

All the same at one point he looked like bringing off his threat. When the flag dropped he went off in front and at the second last was indeed fully a field in front. But his mount was tiring and the other was catching up. To make assurance doubly sure he drove his horse into the second last without reckoning on just how blown he was. The horse turned over on top of him, breaking his pelvis and putting him out of action for the rest of the season. The neighbour, jumping past his prostrate form enquired politely how he was and was he sure what field he was in !

On the visit of the Prince of Wales to Liverpool for the Grand National of 1923 he was appointed his escort and a sort of extra-equerry. When walking the course with HRH before the race and explaining the hazards the Prince asked him what he thought of the various horses and their chances saying that he himself fancied Serjeant Murphy and thought he would have a bet on him. Never slow to express an opinion and that most forcibly, Harry declared : 'Good God, don't do that. He's as old as I am. He's not a horse at all !' When Serjeant Murphy won much as he liked at 100–6 Harry, having seen what was about to happen from two fences out, made himself scarce from the Royal Box.

Always anxious and determined to win he picked his rides with some care avoiding the chancy jumpers and the downright dangerous ones which come to many aspiring to the top, but even so he incurred his share of injury and disaster which happen to every steeplechase rider however accomplished. His brother records that in addition to breaking his pelvis he broke a leg, several ribs, collar bones, two arms and a wrist, the latter so badly that it terminated a career in the saddle that had lasted for no less than twenty-two years.

These injuries, serious though they were, pale into insignificance in comparison to what happened to Frank. He rode his first winner at the age of seventeen. Unlike his brother he would get up on anything. As a result he fractured his skull, had twenty concussions, another suspected fracture at the base of his skull, internal injuries leading to a serious operation, thirteen broken collarbones, a split shin bone, a dislocated shoulder and many minor injuries and knockabouts. Undeterred and undefeated he went on riding until a horse called Sporty Boyee put him into the open ditch at Stratford, trod on him and broke his back.

Shortly before that last accident he had been witness to a splendid piece of skulduggery at the little course at Loughborough. He doesn't say so but he may have taken part in it himself for he seems to have had a remarkably accurate knowledge of the details.

A professional backer owned a horse that appeared to be 'thrown in' to a £300 handicap at the meeting and he and his confrères descended upon it backing the horse off the boards. They were counting their winnings when the horse was seen to be leading by ten lengths at the last.

The judge's stand at that meeting was an old-fashioned sentry box. The little party of professional backers were congregated round it waiting to cheer their horse home and lead him in. But it was not to be. He turned over at the last and came down. Appreciating the disaster that loomed in front of them and the loss of their money the little party took immediate steps to remedy the situation and save their bet. With one accord they advanced on the sentry box. It took only one good push to topple it over with the judge inside. Then to make doubly sure that he could not escape and pronounce a verdict, they sat on it! Once the last runner had passed the post they got up and melted into the crowd.

There being no judge the stewards had no option but to pronounce the race void thus bringing wrath and fury down upon them from the owner and trainer of the actual winner but proving the truth of Frank Brown's words: 'If you can't win, at least you can see to it that you can't lose!'

The professionals had rescued themselves from disaster but

It took only one good push to topple it over with the judge inside.

they had brought it on to the unfortunate judge and officials who were hauled over the coals by the authorities and a permanent judge's box was constructed and safely secured by the time of the next meeting.

Besides Frank and Harry Brown, another pair of brothers enriched the racing scene between the wars. Geoffrey and Quintin (universally known as 'Quinny') Gilbey, scions of the great wine merchant family, were Etonians like the Browns, both destined to become racing journalists of power, prestige and influence.

Geoffrey was the elder and more serious-minded of the two. He knew racing in and out, he was fearless in expressing his opinions and he was the scourge of the evil-doer and the non-trier. Unlike many of his brethren in that era he scorned the soft option of watching the race from the stands or, in many cases during those days, from the bar. Instead, whatever the weather, he would search out and discover irregularities in running and discrepancies in form. Frequently his outspoken comments would bring disaster to the object of his scorn and derision, who had fancied his crimes had been carefully concealed from the stewards on the stands.

Danny Morgan, a very fine steeplechase jockey of that time who amongst other victories won the Champion Hurdle and the Cheltenham Gold Cup was fond of telling how as a young jockey Geoffrey lost him rides for a certain stable.

He had lately come from Ireland and had picked up a chance ride at Worcester where the course lies beside the river Severn. In the parade ring the trainer instructed him to give the horse an easy ride and to be sure not to show him up.

At the last bend Morgan realised to his horror that he was going only too well and that unless he did something and did it quickly it was likely he would be placed at least. All he could think of was to swing as wide as he could round the bend and thus lose ground he would be unable to make up. This he did going so wide in fact that he saw the water flashing by – or he said he did.

Next morning on picking up the newspaper he turned at once to Gilbey's column as the majority of racing people did in those days for he was the most widely read correspondent of his time. To his horror he saw his name figuring prominently in the following passage; 'I have heard stories of how Fred Archer used to come round Tattenham Corner with his left leg over the rails. I was not alive then to witness this feat, but yesterday at Worcester I observed something even more extraordinary for I saw Danny Morgan come round the last bend with his right leg in the River Severn !'

The handicapper took notice and the connections were not amused.

The younger brother, Quinny, was more light-hearted in his approach. After Eton, a short spell in the Guards, and a shorter one in a bank he became what he always wanted to be, a racing journalist. Fond always of wine and women it could have been said of him that he packed twenty-five hours of living into every twenty-four and 'try everything twice' might well have been his motto. By and large a successful gambler nevertheless, as he records, his one foray into bookmaking was an unmitigated disaster. It happened at Gatwick to which he travelled down with his friend, Chubb Leach, who was due to ride a horse called Fair Weather Jack trained by his brother, Felix, in a seller. Chubb told him that Fair Weather Jack had no chance at all against the favourite, Linkman, and that his instructions were to give the horse an easy race. Fair Weather Jack was being shouted at 3–1, and, since he knew the horse had no chance Quinny had the inspiration of turning himself from a backer into a layer. Having decided this he trotted off to a bookmaker and suggested he take a bet of 7–2 against Fair Weather Jack. The bookmaker agreed and the bet was struck at £70–£20. Thinking he was on a certainty, Quinny went off

'. . . I saw Danny Morgan come round the last bend with his right leg in the River Severn !'

to Chubb and reported what he had done saying, 'That's the easiest twenty quid we're ever likely to pick up.'

The race, however, turned out to be even worse than either he or Chubb had expected and, entering the straight, Fair Weather Jack was lying second. Nevertheless, neither thought there was any cause for alarm since Linkman was fully five lengths in front and going easily on the bit. But in a few strides all that changed. Linkman suddenly broke down so badly that he came to a virtual standstill. Leach had no option but to go on and win which, making the best of a bad job, he did in some style with a flourish of his whip.

That was bad enough – £70 of Quinny's, which, as he says, he could ill afford had gone down the chute but, as he also says, the sad story did not end there. Chubb Leach hissed at him as he dismounted to go to the auction and buy in Fair Weather Jack if he went for less than three hundred guineas. This Quinny tried to do but was beaten by another trainer who, taken in by Chubb's fine finish and seeing a prospect in the horse, went far higher in the bidding than they expected.

And still worse was to come. The owner who had only recently joined the stable had been told the horse had no chance and had therefore not bothered to attend the meeting. On being informed that he had won the race and lost his horse he was, not unnaturally, furious, and decided that he had been 'done' by the Leach family or, in plain language, flagrantly cheated. He thereupon removed all his horses and sent them elsewhere. All in all it was quite a day. The money was lost, the horse was lost, the owner was lost and, to complete the story, Fair Weather Jack never won another race.

Quinny also had ambitions as an amateur rider, but his abilities, to say the least of them, never began to rival those of the

Browns. It was another racing journalist, a friend as it happened, who finally exposed them and put him in his place. He owned, in partnership with two others, a horse called Wearing a Crown, which ran in his name. It won a couple of races when ridden by Jack Leach a brother of Chubb's, but then Quinny decided to ride it himself. This resulted in his finishing down the field in the horse's next two outings. After the second defeat he read in the racing column of the *Tatler* the words, penned by that false friend: 'I hear that since Wearing A Crown's owner has taken to riding him in races, the horse's name is to be changed to Carrying a Cross.'

7 Some Grand National Disasters

Not all winners of the Grand National bring fame and fortune with them to their owners, trainers and riders. Sunloch, who won in 1914, is a case in point. In fact his story, though one of apparent success, was nothing but a series of disasters.

Sunloch was cheaply bought for £300 by a Mr Tom Tyler for a man named Willard who became involved in a series of financial troubles – which is putting it politely – that ultimately led to his arrest. Tom Tyler, a bluff sporting yeoman farmer who was a friend of Frank and Harry Brown trained Sunloch for Willard and, after the arrest, he took the horse over to run in his name. Although Sunloch was at the bottom of the handicap, surprisingly enough several interested parties were after him as a National hope, amongst them Sir Charles Assheton Smith who had won the previous two Nationals with Jerry M and Covercoat and was anxious to establish a record by winning a third in succession. Sir Charles made a handsome offer which Tyler refused to his later regret. A generous, open-handed character who loved company, entertained lavishly and lived and betted far beyond his means, by the time the race came round Tyler, like his predecessor, was in some financial difficulty for debts were piling up and creditors were pressing him. He had, however, backed his horse in the ante-post at 100–1.

Sunloch had the minimum weight of 9st 7lb to carry, he was ridden by the largely unknown and inexperienced W. J. Smith and was disregarded in the market. When the tapes went up Smith, making use of his light weight, sent him to the front straightaway. Soon he had a ten length lead and before long

this was increased to twenty lengths. It was a highly unortho-
dox way of riding Aintree and the other jockeys, thinking
nothing of his chances, were content to let him go. In the event
the old racing maxim that you can give away weight but you
cannot give away distance proved only too true for those other
jockeys. Sunloch was never headed and came home alone.

It seemed a triumph and in its way it was but the stake and
his winnings did not last Tom Tyler long. He was over generous in his presents to the jockey and the stable staff, the celebrations were laid on with an even more lavish hand than usual
and stretched from days into weeks. Always a soft touch he
responded only too readily to the spongers and charitable
appeals that follow a famous win. But tomorrow had to come
and come it did. When his creditors, learning of his win, came
crowding down on him there was precious little left of his winnings with which to pay them. Sunloch had to be sold. Sir
Charles Assheton Smith, who had wanted him before, stepped
in and bought him but he did little good for him only winning
one other race, a minor affair at Hawthorn Hill in which he was
ridden by Frank Brown. The proceeds of the sale went to the
creditors. There was nothing left in the stable save a few 'crip-
ples' which were useless and did not win a race. As for Billy
Smith, the jockey, he was held to have ridden a mad race, the
victory did him more harm than good and he got few more
rides. It all added up to Tyler's oft-repeated averment over a
glass that winning that National had been a disaster for them
both and had nearly ruined him.

There were forty-two runners, a record for the race at that
time, in the 1928 Grand National. Amongst them, making his
first appearance in it was Easter Hero, a brilliant bright chest-
nut who already had a reputation for tearaway running and

flamboyant jumping. As was expected he dashed into the lead and blinded the spectators with the speed at which he attacked the big fences – and survived them. All went well until he reached the Canal Turn which then had a ditch at its take-off side. For reasons best known to himself possibly because he was going too fast at the turn, Easter Hero decided to run down this fence. His rider managed to straighten him and, facing it, he then put in a stupendous leap. He was, however, unbalanced and meeting it all wrong and he landed slap on top of it.

So far in front was Easter Hero that he was able to carry out this performance by himself. The next thing to happen to him was that he fell backwards into the ditch. Having arrived at the bottom somehow on his feet he then ran down it trying to get out.

By this time the rest of the field had arrived and the spectacle of Easter Hero prancing in the ditch was too much for most of them. At least half the huge field either refused or fell in trying to avoid him. In the mêlée of swerving, refusing and falling horses, cursing jockeys and flying hooves some of the bravest of the brave tried again. Mr J. B. Balding on his own horse Drinmod, put him at the fence eight times before giving up.

One of the few lucky ones was the American horse Billy Barton who had managed to jump both Easter Hero and the fence. An unconsidered outsider, the tubed Tipperary Tim, had somehow got away with it too and coming to the second last these two along with Great Span were together with Great Span apparently going the better of the three. But disaster was far from done with yet. Great Span's saddle slipped as he took off giving his jockey no chance of staying with him and he was out of the race.

That left Tipperary Tim and Billy Barton alone at the last. Billy Barton was being shouted home a winner when he, too, tiring, came down. Tipperary Tim romped home alone at 66–1. Billy Barton was remounted to take second place. There were no other finishers. After this victory Tipperary Tim, in

Mr J. B. Balding on his own horse Drinmod, put him at the fence eight times
before giving up.

the words of one commentator, 'returned to the obscurity from whence he came'.

Until the appearance of Arkle on the steeplechasing scene Golden Miller was universally acknowledged as the greatest steeplechaser ever and it is still a matter of speculation, especially amongst that dwindling number of the older generation who saw him race, whether he or Arkle was, in fact, the greater. He won five Cheltenham Gold Cups and won the Gold Cup and the Grand National in the same year, 1934, feats which have never been equalled nor are they likely to be and will probably stand for all time. In 1935 he survived a terribly hard race against Thomond II in the Gold Cup to go on to Liverpool as the shortest priced favourite at 2–1 in the Grand National.

Golden Miller was owned by the eccentric millionairess, Dorothy Paget, who was fond of betting, her own sex and meals taken at night mostly consisting of fish and chips despite the fact that she kept in constant employment a 'night cook.' Her dislikes were men, losing and the majority of her trainers and jockeys. In 1935 and for some years prior to that her horses were trained by Basil Briscoe a highly strung young man, son of a wealthy father who had come to training by way of Eton and Cambridge. Briscoe, always immaculately turned out in tweeds and a trilby, and Miss Paget in her battered beret and shabby old coat, which were her invariable wear on the racecourse, were an ill-assorted pair. But they shared one thing at least – a fondness for betting. Both loved a gamble and both plunged heavily and it was this which may well have been the major element in the rift that was soon and sensationally to develop between them.

It all really began with that race for the Gold Cup. Briscoe, anticipating that no one would take his champion on had been comparatively easy with Golden Miller in his preparation for this race aiming to bring him to his peak at Liverpool. He was horrified when he heard only a few hours before the race that Miss Paget's cousin, J. H. Whitney, had decided to run his very good horse, Thomond II, for Thomond II had the previous year inflicted one of his few defeats on Golden Miller when in receipt of only 7lb.

The story of that Gold Cup needs no retelling here save only to relate that Golden Miller had to run for his life and give everything he had in the hardest race of his career which has gone down in history as the steeplechase of the century, and he was not really ready for it. If he was not distressed as he stood in the winner's enclosure he was as near to it as he ever was. One commentator indeed, remarked that Miss Paget had been taking longer steps than he was as she led him in.

Between the Gold Cup and the Grand National stories became current that Golden Miller had not fully recovered from that hard race and, moreover, that Briscoe, who was frequently accused of over-galloping his horses, was doing just that to him now and putting him through some searching tests. These stories did not deter the general public from backing him and he was to start the race at 2–1, the hottest favourite in the history of the race. Miss Paget, however, had heard them and taken heed of them. When she saw the horse she expressed her opinion of his looks and condition in no uncertain fashion to her trainer.

Briscoe was, as has been said, a highly strung man. The responsibility, the doubts about the full recovery of the great horse in his care coupled with threats to the horse's safety and rumours of nobbling which were coming to him must have tightened the strain on his nerves. There was, too, the money factor. He had backed Golden Miller to win him £10,000 and since he knew that Miss Paget's minimum bet on anything she fancied was in the region of £2,000 he must have known, too, that her stake in the race was colossal.

There was something else as well. Golden Miller was alone

103

among her many horses to touch Miss Paget's strange affections – after one of his wins she had actually and uncharacteristically greeted him with a smacking kiss. One observer, on seeing this remarked that it was the first time she had ever kissed a member of the opposite sex. On hearing him a friend standing by said: 'And he's a gelding.'

All these things considered Briscoe would have been wiser to have returned a soft answer to her complaints but his temperament would not permit him to do so. He flared up and told Miss Paget if that was how she felt she should have her horses trained elsewhere.

Brushes between owner and trainer when nerves are stretched and expectations great are by no means unheard of and all might have been well had Golden Miller lived up to his reputation. At first he looked like doing so taking all the early fences, including the dreaded Beechers, where he had pitched dangerously once before, clearly and with all his own authority. He cleared the Canal Turn with the race, so far as could be said at that stage, apparently in his keeping. But at the second fence after Valentines, an open ditch, disaster occurred.

No one knows just what happened for there are multitudes of explanations and opinions all of them differing, and it is, at this distance of time, fruitless to indulge in speculation. What is certain is that Golden Miller, while he did not fall, made a mess of the jump, and got rid of his jockey. Without him the heart went out of the race.

Never, probably, in the history of steeplechasing has the disappearance of the favourite caused such a sensation or brought such a series of disasters in its train. On his return Wilson maintained that the horse had never been right, had not given him a proper feel throughout the race and he thought he was lame. These sentiments did not endear him to his trainer.

An immense amount of money had been lost not least by those two closest to the horse, Briscoe and Miss Paget. With Miss Paget it was not so much the losing of the money that hurt, though that was bad enough, but the disappointment of

. . . it was the first time she had ever kissed a member of the opposite sex.

defeat which entailed in some odd way loss of face, especially where the horse was her beloved Golden Miller and the fall such a questionable one. Nevertheless, to Briscoe's dismay, she appeared to accept all that Wilson had said, which, he considered, reflected on his training.

A furious slanging match developed between them in Miss Paget's box in the course of which, according to one who was there and soon made himself scarce, Briscoe hurled his gold cigarette case against the door shouting: 'Well, then take your bloody horse away!'

After much discussion, most of it acrimonious, on the advice of the vets who could find nothing wrong with the horse, Golden Miller started in the Champion Chase the next day. He hit the very first fence so hard that no jockey could have had a hope of staying in the saddle and once again he got rid of Wilson.

More recriminations followed, many of them in public through statements made by leading actors in the drama. Briscoe, as is the way with certain of the highly-strung, was by then driven beyond all reason. He seemed determined to push himself into a pit of his own making and lose the great horse for whom he had done so much. He wrote to Miss Paget telling her that all her horses must be out of his yard within a week and he made the letter known to the press. In four days they were gone.

Golden Miller, though he won one more Gold Cup was never the same horse again. After he lost him and Miss Paget's other horses Briscoe had to move to smaller quarters and his career went into a decline. A friend recorded how in the great days of Golden Miller's career his massive gambles had brought him a credit of £35,000. The friend, who had connections in the city, implored him to invest at least the larger part of it. Briscoe refused saying that the previous week he had picked up £7,000 betting so why should he lock money away? Finally, the friend records, 'he lost the lot'.

Sadly he lost much else besides. His life thereafter was a series of disasters into which it is not necessary to enter now.

He died, aged forty-eight, a broken man, on 21 August 1951.

For nearly a decade after the Second World War and before his tragic early death, Lord Mildmay of Flete was the best liked, most respected and one of the most effective amateur riders of his day. As John Hislop, a friend and fellow-rider, wrote of him after his death, 'he was the foremost figure in steeplechasing today and the very personification of its true spirit'.

In 1936, however, as the Honourable Anthony Mildmay, he was only a beginner at the game but his greatest ambition was then and always remained to ride the winner of the Grand National. A bad fall in the Foxhunter's Chase the year before, which had kept him out of the saddle some time, had not quelled his ardour nor lessened that aim.

Shortly before the National of 1936 came round his father, the then Lord Mildmay, had bought for him to ride in it a tubed gelding called Davy Jones for the modest sum of £650. Davy Jones was by Pharos, he was bred for the flat at which he had proved useless and had been even more cheaply bought as a Newmarket 'throw-out' by a Mr Tom Rayson. When he brought him home Mr Rayson found to his astonishment that he was a natural jumper and it was on his recommendation that Lord Mildmay bought him as a safe conveyance for his son round Liverpool since memory of that bad fall was still fresh in the father's mind.

When he was thrown up in the parade ring before the race for reason which has never been fully explained Mildmay did not tie the knot in his reins which is usually done by jockeys to make them secure. This may have been due to pre-National nerves which affect even the most hardened riders and Mildmay at that stage of his career was far from being one of these

107

or, as has been suggested, he did it deliberately so as to be able to slip his reins further at the drop fences. Whether accidental or deliberate for this omission he was to pay a high price.

Golden Miller was again in the field and, despite the happenings of the year before and the fact that he had 12st 7lb to carry, he was made second favourite to Mrs Mundy's brilliant young horse, Avenger. Davy Jones was amongst the forgotten no-hopers at 100–1.

At the very first fence Golden Miller put paid to the hopes of those who had backed him and were looking to his rehabilitation for he was brought down by a French challenger falling in front of him. And then, as the race progressed, to the astonishment of all, Davy Jones proceeded to give a breathtaking display of how to tackle the great Aintree fences. His jumping was fast and free and unblemished by mistakes even at the dreaded drops. When they finished the first circuit and came to the water opposite the stands he was lying second to Avenger and out-jumping him. At the next fence Avenger fell, breaking his neck, the first great disaster of the race. That left Davy Jones in front and there he stayed, still flinging great leaps, horse and rider enjoying every minute of it. On reaching the racecourse Davy Jones was fully ten lengths ahead of a tiring Reynoldstown, the previous year's winner, whose rider had lost his whip. At the second last Davy Jones was still full of running and victory must have seemed secure in his young rider's grasp. At this fence Davy Jones made his one and only mistake and that a slight one. But to make certain of his recovery Mildmay slipped the reins through his fingers. And then the awful, the unspeakable happened.

The tongue of the buckle either broke or pulled through the retaining bar. The reins, unknotted, parted, leaving his rider powerless to guide or control his mount. Mildmay made an effort to keep him straight with his whip but it was hopeless. Davy Jones swerved past the last fence and went off the course and out of the race. It was over. The prize had been torn from his grasp. Those bright thoughts of victory in the greatest steeplechase of all had vanished in a few strides. It is not surprising that his rider confessed that night that he felt like throwing himself into the Mersey.

And, as frequently happens, the fates, having once snatched away a much wanted prize, never relented. Although, after war service, Davy Jones's rider now himself Lord Mildmay of Flete, came back to become a leading amateur and to head the list of winning amateur riders he never succeeded in wiping out the memory of that disaster by winning the great race. Once again the prize seemed almost his; once again the fates intervened. In 1948 he was well fancied and well handicapped on his own horse, Cromwell. Kicked before the start Cromwell jumped sluggishly in the early stages and Mildmay had to drive him into his fences. But at Valentines second time round where the final stages of the race begin to take their shape, he was with the leaders. Moving easily and jumping cleanly, he appeared to have as good if not a better chance than anyone.

And then, once more disaster came. In a bad fall at Folkestone earlier in the season Mildmay had broken his neck. One result of this injury was that the neck muscles were prone to 'freeze', locking the head in one position. As Cromwell and his rider landed over the third last, one of the most critical moments in the race, this is what happened. From that fence onward Mildmay's chin was locked against his chest and he could neither raise nor move his head. There was nothing he could do to help his horse and he could, in fact, scarcely see where he was going. It is a tribute to his skill and courage that he managed to keep in the race at all, finishing third whereas if this had not happened he must have been much closer and might well have won. So, once more, he was cruelly robbed if not of the race itself at least of his chance of winning it.

Two years later Lord Mildmay was tragically drowned while swimming near his Devonshire home. He was a great Corinthian and a great sportsman. Truly indeed was it said of him: 'There was never a harder rider, a better loser or a more popular winner.'

> For all sad words of tongue or pen,
> The saddest are these : 'It might have been.'

Those words of the poet might have echoed and echoed again through Dick Francis's brain on the night of the Grand National of 1956.

Dick Francis is so famous now as the author of a series of enormously successful racing thrillers that it is sometimes forgotten that he had an earlier equally successful career as a steeplechase jockey and was champion in 1953–54. That was the year in which he landed the plum job of first jockey to the powerful stable of P.V.F. Cazalet who trained for many of the great names in steeplechasing, including HM the Queen Mother.

In Cazalet's stable was a big, strapping brown horse belonging to the Queen Mother called Devon Loch. In 1956 he was quietly fancied for the Grand National and Francis looked forward eagerly to riding him in it. In the race his expectations were more than justified. Everything went right for him, the horse jumped beautifully, suffered no interference and on the second circuit he had, as he records, 'the sort of run one dreams about'.

Coming to the last, Devon Loch was still going as well as ever and still on the bridle while the only horses near him were hard ridden. He jumped the fence cleanly and began the long run in, his race apparently in safe keeping, his rider poised and confident that he was about to record a Royal victory. The crowd thought so, too. As Devon Loch strode up the straight they rose to their feet and a storm of cheering erupted from the stands. Nothing like it had ever been heard at Aintree before. Hats were already coming off ; some went up in the air.

Then – disaster of disasters occurred. Devon Loch, who had jumped those mighty fences without the semblance of a mistake, suddenly checked in his gallop, sprawled and a second later was down – on the flat. It was in fact more a collapse than a fall and it left his rider no hope of helping him. He was out of the race with the winning post only fifty yards away. It was unbelievable but the unbelievable had happened. Heartbroken, Francis threw his whip on the ground ; tears were not far away from him. Fate had robbed him of the greatest prize a steeplechase jockey can have at the very moment, almost, of his triumph.

It has been called, rightly, 'the saddest of all Nationals'. And to this day no one knows what went wrong or brought about that collapse. Many theories have been advanced. Some say Devon Loch tried to jump an imaginary fence and, like a human treading on a stair 'that isn't there' sprawled and came down, others that his action, never his strongest point, betrayed him on that long run in and that he 'tripped over himself', as it were, and so fell.

Francis's own explanation appears to be the most likely. He maintains that the massive volume of cheering which met horse and rider in the straight and which was, he says, in its strength and intensity far greater than anything he had ever before experienced, hit Devon Loch almost as if he had run into a wall. In response the horse to save himself attempted to throw himself backwards, became entirely unbalanced and so came down.

Bad luck, as so often happens, brings one disaster after another. Within a year Devon Loch had broken down so badly it was clear he would never race again and a succession of bad falls had led to Francis retiring from the saddle. At least he could console himself with the thought : 'I know what it is like to win the National, even though I did not do it' – something which no other man in racing history has been able to say. Though, for him, even this reassurance was clouded when, as he records, he heard 'one man say to another a little while ago,

111

"Who did you say that was? Dick Francis? Oh, yes, he's the man who didn't win the National." What an epitaph !'

But when he wrote those words Francis had not started his second career. He will, in fact, always be remembered as the man who triumphantly survived that terrible disaster followed by enforced retirement from a game he loved to become world famous in another sphere. His books have brought pleasure to millions, profit to himself, and earned him a unique niche in the writing pantheon of the present half-century.

8 *Tricking the Books*

Many are the devices conjured up by those anxious to turn an easy penny and to deprive bookmakers of what they consider to be their ill-gotten gains, but most of them, one way or another, have ended in disaster for their perpetrators.

Possibly the most ingenious and audacious of all such schemes was what became known as the Trodmore Affair which took place before the First World War. Just who its originators were was never discovered though it ended in financial disaster for the plotters due to the astuteness of one bookmaker.

George Somers along with his brother, Charles, carried on a Turf Accountant business under the name of Coulson & Co. Why they were selected to carry the bulk of the bets by those determined to defraud them is not clear but it may have been because they did not occupy a place on the rails but walked about the ring taking bets and thus it was thought that placing the money with them would attract less publicity.

At all events during a Bank Holiday Meeting at Hurst Park a client came to George Somers and struck away bets with him, two at Ripon and three at Trodmore Park. All were substantial starting price wagers. Somers, who had never heard of Trodmore Park, queried these bets. The client told him there was indeed a meeting there that day and advised him to look in the current issue of *The Sportsman*, then the most widely read racing daily, if he doubted it. Somers consulted his copy of *The Sportsman* and did indeed find it all there in black and white, a complete programme with names of races, distances, weights and probable starters amongst whom were the three horses named by the client. Reassured, Somers took the bets. Next day he found they had all won at prices of 2–1, 3–1 and 5–1.

Somers had had a sizeable loss and he was still far from happy about the whole transaction. He had never heard of Trodmore and despite the information contained in *The Sportsman* his instinct born of years of experience told him that something was wrong. When the client came to collect he asked him just where Trodmore was. The reply was vague in the extreme – somewhere near St Ives, the client said. Somers, still suspicious, then told him that he was withholding payment until he had checked out the whereabouts of Trodmore Park and if a race meeting had in fact taken place there that day. The client protested saying that he had every right to be paid and finally departed issuing threats of reporting Somers to Tattersalls if payment was not made.

Having consulted a directory Somers found that there were two St Ives, one in Huntingdon, and the other in Cornwall. He then sent telegrams to the Post Offices and police in both cases asking if such a race meeting as Trodmore Park existed in their area, and, to make doubly sure, if racing anywhere had taken place on the day in question within fifty miles of them. The answer came back immediately. There was no such place as Trodmore Park nor had a meeting of any sort been held within the radius requested by Somers.

On receiving this information Somers indignantly sent it on to *The Sportsman* asking for an explanation why they had published details of a fictitious meeting. The enquiry threw the staff into a panic and an investigation took place. It transpired that the plotters had chosen their day well and carried out their work cleverly. On a bank holiday there were so many meetings that checking was not as thorough as usual and therefore the notification had slipped through. Moreover – it looked right. The details were set out just as were genuine ones and were done on official paper exactly as if prepared and submitted by an authentic clerk of the course. The editor, of course, with a very red face, had to admit their error and contemplate damages which he was very fortunate not to pay for Somers had meanwhile notified the police and the 'client' never came to claim his money, nor, needless to say, to report him to Tattersalls.

It was an ingenious and daring fraud which almost came off. Whoever was responsible must have had a thorough knowledge of racing and the racing press for their fictitious meeting was well presented and accurately framed. They were never traced though several names were mentioned as the perpetrators by those in the know. Somers's 'client' vanished. His name, too, was as false as Trodmore Park.

The ingenuity of those who planned the Trodmore Park affair was worthy of a better cause though there are those who say there cannot be a better cause than cheating bookmakers. One of them who was unquestionably holding such sentiments was Peter Christian Barrie, king of the 'ringers'. A 'ringer' for the benefit of the uninitiated is a good horse run in the name of a bad one. It was Barrie who coined the immortal phrase from the dock when at last brought to book and asked by the magistrate in the committal proceedings what he considered to be a good thing in racing: 'A useful three-year-old in a moderate two-year-old race, your honour.'

In many ways a likeable rogue, Barrie specialised in running 'ringers', backing them heavily and whisking them away after they had won and before they could be identified by the authorities. On occasion the appearance of the 'useful' animal had to be altered to make it conform at least in some degree with that of the dud, but a small matter like that did not deter Barrie. He had made up a special dye to obscure markings and on one occasion at least used it to paint a mare all over, converting her from bay with a white blaze to brown with no markings at all. He did this so thoroughly that he had great difficulty in removing the dye to bring the mare back to her natural colour after she had won. First he tried washing her all over with petrol, a drastic enough remedy one might have thought, but it did not work. He then procured a dozen bottles of peroxide and set to work with them. Surprised at this task by the trainer with whom he was boarding the mare he explained what he was doing by saying she had become hot after a gallop and he was attempting to cool her with some 'new American bath wash' which had adhered to her coat and wouldn't come off. He was always a ready, fluent and convincing liar and he had as well an air of disarming innocence about him which enabled him to get away with the most outlandish stories and to land several staggering coups.

But, like many of his kind, Barrie became careless and outreached himself. He was, besides, too greedy. As well as diddling the authorities he withheld their share from some of the accomplices whom he had to have for the successful carrying out of his schemes. They began to complain, and, worse still, to talk. Belatedly the authorities began to take notice of what was going on and to get on his track. 'Tricky' Drew, of whom we have heard before, was one of those employed to investigate him. With his underworld and racing contacts he began to ferret out the truth.

Barrie's run of success, meanwhile, was beginning to come to an end through a mixture of over-confidence and bad luck. Two of his ringers were unexpectedly beaten with the result that money was running out. He could not pay to ship them abroad where they would be away from all surveillance or identification. He had therefore to keep them on his premises and when an Inspector from Scotland Yard arrived there he could not explain their presence nor give an adequate explanation of just what and who they were. It soon became clear that they were not what he claimed them to be and that they had run under false names. Disaster followed. He was arrested, tried on charges of fraud and sentenced to three years with hard labour.

But it was hard to keep Barrie down. When he came out he

. . . converting her from bay with a white blaze to brown with no markings at all.

became what perhaps he was well qualified to be – a racing tipster. He was never anything else but plausible and for a while his business flourished. Somehow he managed to collect and number amongst his clients all sorts of respectable people, clergymen and the like who wanted their investments kept confidential and communication with them to be by way of plain envelopes. Unfortunately for him Edgar Wallace, the famous crime novelist, discovered him and, after writing his life story, insisted on becoming a partner in the business.

Wallace loved racing, the horses, the characters, the excitements, and all its ups and downs. But he thought he knew everything about it when in fact he knew nothing and never took the trouble to learn its wiles and its ways. When he became a partner he took over the 'tipping' end of the business. Since he had squandered one if not two fortunes himself backing losers he was not likely to be more successful when advising others. Soon the plain envelopes were winging away from over the stable in Brick Lane, Piccadilly where the business was conducted, carrying the most improbable selections and recommendations. 'Angry complaints', Wallace's biographer records, came crowding back, 'of horses that were unplaced, of club funds and life's savings lost.'

Once more disaster stared Barrie in the face, for Wallace was ruining the fine little business he had built up. He dissolved the partnership, politely dispensed with Wallace's services and tried to salvage what he could from the wreck.

Wallace went away to back more losers of his own and to invest more money in useless horses whom he always thought were going to win him a classic. But his association with Barrie had given him the material for the series of stories about Educated Evans, the cockney tipster whose character and activities are based on Barrie, so in the end that engaging rogue gained some sort of immortality.

9 Old Guts and Gaiters

For no very clearly discernible reason the first Lord Glanely, formerly plain James Tatem who had fought his way up from a shipping clerk to control a vast fleet and amass a huge fortune, was known to the racing public between the wars as 'old guts and gaiters'. A big florid man with a walrus moustache and a rough tongue he spent an immense amount of money on bloodstock, much of it showing little or no return. A familiar figure at every Tattersalls auction, vendors would search eagerly for his presence in the ring when about to introduce their products since he invariably strengthened the market and if he cast his eye on anything he specially fancied might well send it sky-high. Racing and cricket were his two passions in life and he was inclined to impatience with his jockeys and his players.

One day he turned up at a sale wearing immaculate white ducks and spotless buckskin shoes. Feeling that he needed some strengthening before he advanced to do battle in the sales ring he repaired to the bar and ordered a bottle of champagne. Once it was placed before him he took his time over its consumption and studied the catalogue.

While this was going on one vendor especially was growing more and more anxious at his absence. He was in need of a good sale and felt that the best of his lot had the breeding and appearance to appeal to his lordship. But time went inexorably on and still Old Guts and Gaiters did not appear. News that he was in the bar and apparently entrenched there behind a bottle of champagne was conveyed to the vendor. 'He must have had the hell of a night last night,' the vendor said to a friend, 'or else he'd be here. What am I to do?'

. . . he was in the bar and apparently entrenched there behind a bottle of champagne. . .

'You've only one course left to you,' was the advice he received. 'The bar is made of wood. Go down and set fire to it and smoke the old bugger out!'

Fortunately for all concerned this proved unnecessary. The bottle was finished just in time and to the relief of all the vendors present the old man appeared. Majestically, clad all in white, he left the bar and strode to his accustomed place to be greeted by the auctioneer with the words: 'And which end will you open the bowling from, my lord?'

He paid top price for that nervous vendor's lot but, like many of his high-priced yearlings, it did not turn out a success. In 1934, however, it looked as if luck was running his way at last. His colt Colombo had been winter favourite for the Derby and appeared to have every chance of giving him his second Epsom vistory, the first having been achieved with Grand Parade in 1919, fifteen years before. When Colombo won the Two Thousand Guineas he was hailed in most quarters as a world beater and backed as a certainty for the Derby.

There were some, however, who pointed to his dam's pedigree and wondered if he would stay the Derby distance; others had their doubts about his owner's wisdom in going to France for his jockey, and overlooking the claims or expectations of Steve Donoghue who had ridden Colombo in most of his two-year-old races. Donoghue was as outstanding round Epsom as Archer had been before him and Piggott was to be after him while Rae Johnstone, an Australian riding in France on whom the choice fell, though a brilliant jockey had little experience of the Derby and its difficulties.

Lord Glanely, however, had no doubts about the outcome. He backed Colombo heavily as was his wont with one of his fancied runners and he went to the extent of tempting fate by ordering a celebratory dinner to be prepared for him in his favourite restaurant before taking himself off to Epsom. Such over-confidence often brings disaster in its train and in this case it did.

Colombo was beaten. It was one of the most sensational defeats of the century. Money had poured on to Colombo from here, there and everywhere right up to the off and he was backed by both punters and cognoscenti as if defeat was out of the question. He suffered interference in running whether deliberate or accidental no one now can say and could only finish third.

A storm burst about the unfortunate Johnstone's head. He was blamed for getting shut in, for staying on the rails too long, for having to come round a wall of horses – for everything. His own opinion backed up by a few good judges, among them Quintin Gilbey, was that Colombo just didn't stay and would have been beaten anyway but he hardly helped his case by confining himself in public to the one laconic comment: 'At least no lives were lost.'

Old Guts and Gaiters reacted explosively. His language was always uninhibited. Once when his jockey wanted to object the day after the stewards had had words with him about the running of one of his horses his reply was: 'Not bloody likely. I saw enough of those buggers yesterday to last me a lifetime.' No one knows what passed between him and Johnstone but the outcome was all but inevitable. He cancelled Johnstone's retainer and fired him as his first jockey; he never won another Derby.

It was for all concerned a disaster of the first magnitude and one wonders who attended to eat that 'celebration' dinner. Johnstone would hardly have been the guest of honour.

10   *Tailpieces*

Starts can have their disasters just as much as finishes. This was especially so before starting stalls became universal and gates were used – and when the starter was autocratic. Many are the stories told of the wiles employed by jockeys at the gate when they wished to get a good start – or a bad one.

A leading Australian jockey in the days of starting gates, whom we shall call Brown, was well known to the starter for his tactic of keeping behind his field and then creeping up, watching the starter's hand on the lever all the time. This ensured that he was on the move when the hand went down and the gate went up. As a result he could all but anticipate the start and get what was then known as 'a flyer from the gate'. The starter did not care for this and it became a battle of wits between the two of them both of whom, as it happened, were keen and spirited poker players.

Eventually the starter decided to put a stop, once and for all, to Brown's activities at the gate and, waiting on his rostrum to start a big handicap, singled him out. 'Come along, Brown, get your horse into line', he called out. 'I can't get him up, sir', was the reply.

The following dialogue then took place :

STARTER: All right, then, pay a fiver when you get back to the weighing room.
BROWN: What for, sir?
STARTER: Pay a tenner, Brown.
BROWN: But I haven't done anything wrong, sir!
STARTER: Pay fifteen, Brown.

BROWN: Right, sir, I'll *see* you!

There is no prize for guessing what happened to Brown in the stewards' room when he did get back.

Sex, as we all know, plays a part in every walk of life and in racing, too, it can upset the best laid plans. The Earl of Carnarvon tells a story against himself in his younger days as a gentleman rider. He was due to ride a horse of his own called Lights o' London at an Ayr meeting. A professional backer with whom he was friendly asked him if he thought he had a chance and whether it was worth his while travelling to Ayr to back him. Carnarvon, or Porchester as he was then, assured him that Lights o' London was in with a great chance, should win and advised a substantial investment. He himself, he said, was having a good bet.

Carnarvon was due to travel north on the sleeper from Euston. On his way to the station he decided that he had time on hand and, never averse to the real lights o' London himself, dropped in at the Embassy Club then the resort of all the well-heeled young and lovely in the metropolis. There he met a delightful girl who told him she was bored with the company she was in and very soon she was agreeing to share his sleeping car on the journey north.

Lights o' London was a horse that needed riding. He had only one run and required to be covered up during a race until the time came to produce it. On his arrival at the racecourse after his night in the sleeper the noble Lord felt that he was not at his best, to use his own words: 'Lights o' London was in good shape, in fact, far better than his owner-rider.' The upshot was that Lights o' London took charge some distance out and went for home far earlier than he should have done or than his rider wanted. He was beaten half a length in a race he

'Lights o' London was in good shape, in fact, far better than his owner–
rider.'

should have had at his mercy. Carnarvon had lost his own money but far worse he had also lost his friend's who descended upon him voicing his opinion about the race he had ridden and not mincing his words. This is what came singing about Carnarvon's ears: 'What on earth's the matter with you? Are you bloody well crazy? You look like the wrath of God and I expect you were up to no good last night which accounted for your riding such an awful race.'

'I told him', Lord Carnarvon says. 'That he was perfectly correct!'

Nights of love are sometimes dearly paid for.

Shortly after the last war there was a lot of hot money about a leading North country jockey who was due to ride the outright favourite in a three mile chase at a Yorkshire meeting. After he had changed a message came to him that someone wanted to see him and was waiting outside the back door to the weigh room which was used by jockeys and officials.

Going out he found a character standing by with his hat pulled down over his eyes, the collar of his raincoat turned up round his ears and a large suitcase in his hand. Beckoning him over the character turned a little to one side and opened the suitcase an inch or two so that the jockey could see the contents. It was packed with high-denomination notes.

'These are all yours', the character said, 'if you stop the favourite.'

The jockey told him to go to hell and returned to the weigh room.

The favourite fell at the first fence.

At Newton Abbot on 28 August 1984, Mr Stuart Kittow went out to ride Tango Shandy in a novice chase. Such races are risky events both for man and horse and this one was no exception. The other runners had disappeared for one reason or another save for himself and Legal Session, when the latter fell some distance from home and he looked to have the race at his mercy. Approaching the last, however, fate took a hand for his saddle slipped. Unsighted through no fault of his rider, the horse made a dreadful mistake at that final fence and was all but on the floor. Mr Kittow lost his irons; the saddle was askew; it was a miracle he did not fall off, and Tango Shandy galloped on with his rider more or less round his neck. Somehow Mr Stuart Kittow got back on top and continued without any saddle at all. But the effort had been too much. Just before the line he slipped, came unstuck and hit the ground. Undaunted Mr Kittow held on to the reins and was dragged across the finishing line. No other runner was near enough to challenge, for Legal Session, himself having been remounted, was a very far-away second.

Having crossed the line in front together with his horse, albeit that the connection was a tenuous one, Mr Kittow considered himself the winner; as did the judge who awarded him the race and his name went up in the frame. The local stewards, however, took a different view. They held that as the fall had taken place before the finish, the race was not his and disqualified him. This result was greeted with dismay and disappointment, not only by Mr Kittow, but also by the sporting crowd, who had lustily cheered him home and were delighted to see guts and determination justly, as they thought, rewarded.

It was indeed, as Sir John Astley would have said, 'cruel hard luck', and had it not been for that decision Mr Kittow could well have gone down into history along with a famous old-time amateur, Arthur Yates, who suffered a somewhat similar calamity. Yates, however, held on by the tail and used it to assist him to remount while his horse was galloping on, inspiring the jingle:

In racing reports it is oft-time said
A jockey has cleverly won by a head,
But Yates has performed, when all other arts fail,
A more wonderful feat, for he won by a *tail*.

There is, however, a happy ending of sorts, for the bets, if there were any, were allowed to stand. On appeal to the Jockey Club, it was held that the judge was correct and the decision of the local stewards was reversed.